For Joanna, a townie who mad
and taught me to see beauty

A Wiltshire Year: the history of England in one county First published 2017 by Benzina publishing, LHG Kings Road, Easterton, SN10 4PX

ISBN 978-0-9932583-2-69

Printed by Cambrian Printers

BY THE SAME AUTHOR

MOTO GUZZI - THE COMPLETE STORY

DUCATI DESMODUE

HONDA V4

DUCATI & THE TT

A Wiltshire Year

THE HISTORY *of* ENGLAND *in* ONE COUNTY

by

GREG PULLEN

CONTENTS

- INTRODUCTION -

Years ago I learnt not to bother telling people that I live in Wiltshire. It usually just gets a blank look. So I took to telling them I live near Stonehenge. Most people, even Americans, can conjure up Stonehenge in their mind's eye.

When our kids went to university, they quickly adopted the same trick. But the list of places we could also use makes you wonder how Wiltshire remains hidden in plain sight. To live in Wiltshire means to live near Salisbury Cathedral. Near Avebury stone circle. Near Lacock, where countless period dramas and Harry Potter were filmed. Near where the world's most famous canoe race starts. Near where Brunel based his Great Western Railways. Where crop circles appear. Where Wadworth's beer is brewed and Dyson is based. Where the white horses are carved into chalk hillsides. Where the greatest cavalry battle of the English Civil War was fought. Near Longleat safari park. Near where the Army train on Salisbury Plain, the wildest, most untouched, open grassland in Europe. You know, the vast open vistas that surround the A303, that you only see through a car windscreen as you shuffle between the south east and Cornwall. The bit where you pass Stonehenge. That is Wiltshire. It is been my home for the last fifty years, and I promise you it is the most wonderful place to live on earth.

Walking the dog, up on the Wessex Ridgeway, I can see everywhere I've lived since 1968. Is this a good thing, to have seen so much of one place, risking the loss of a better life somewhere else? Perhaps, and I certainly thought so as a teenager stranded in what seemed like a rural wasteland, peering into a brighter world through the prism of the BBC's Radio 1 and motorcycle magazines.

But then I started to travel and work around the world and came to realise my discontent was connected more to a lack of transport rather than where I lived. And now I think this probably is one of the best places in the world to live, especially if you like a bit of social history. And, unlike villages, towns and cities the landscape of the countryside does not really change – the seasons have more of an effect than the years. In villages house names such as The Old Post Office and The Old Vicarage tell of changing times, while the homogenisation of high streets, as the big chains of restaurants and retailers move in, dilutes and alters the character of towns and cities. But up on the ancient droving route that is the Ridgeway you can trace human civilisation from its beginnings to the highest of today's high tech in one seamless sweep.

Wiltshire is one of the least populous counties in England, ironic given that it was the most densely populated place in the UK when Stonehenge was built. And although you can not see Stonehenge from the Ridgeway, it is only ten miles away. Ten miles in the opposite direction is the even more impressive Avebury, Stonehenge's World Heritage Site sibling. Avebury is where the science of archaeology started, back in the eighteenth century, some 5000 years after it was built.

Below the downs in the middle distance is Devizes, built on an easily defended promontory, with one of the finest Norman street plans and churches in the country. There are also the remains of the castle that marked the divide – hence Devizes – between the manors of crown and church.

The church's centre of power in these parts was down in Salisbury, where the cathedral was built in a single style and at great speed, in just 38 years, when most cathedrals took over a century to build. It is home to one of the Magna Cartas, the document that started to limit the crown and state's power over its people.

The other market towns are further away from the Ridgeway, following rivers. They are punctuated at roughly ten mile intervals, that being a reasonable day's travel if droving livestock, or travelling to and from an outlying village. Rivers are an obvious place to settle, easy to travel along and with eels and fish to catch. Later on they were useful for processing sheep fleeces into wool and cloth. But the first people to settle here lived up on top of the downs, building hill forts and terraces known as strip lynchets: there is one just a few hundred yards from where I climb up to the Ridgeway. The high chalk downs – so called after an old English word, dun, meaning hill – had soil just few inches deep, discouraging trees from growing up here. The valleys below were heavily wooded and home to bears and wolves, so trips down to collect water and firewood were fraught with danger. The downs may have been safer but there is no source of water on the porous chalk, although the thin soil does mean you can carve impressive white horses onto slopes that can be seen for miles around. The one I can see above Devizes was created for the millennium, but most are a few hundred years old.

The steep slopes made these lands easily watched over and defended, but it is a double edged sword. The steep, rounded rise near Devizes is Oliver's Castle, scene of a battle in the English Civil War, arguably the bloodiest war in human history. The Royalist cavalry forced the mounted Parliamentarians back to the slope where they had to stand and fight, or tumble down several hundred feet of almost unclimbable grassland. The place they fell became known as Bloody Ditch, such were their losses.

Further to the west there is West Lavington (naming settlements was not something people fretted over unduly) with its church set almost below the strip lynchets. Above it is the village's plague pit. The plagues killed a third of England's population, and mass graves near churches – and so consecrated ground – were the only way to cope. This is the reason churches are rarely where you would expect them, in the centre of a village, but more often on the edges of villages, next to open countryside, as fearful locals moved away from the burial sites.

Gradually human activity cleared the woodland that covered Wiltshire's plains and valleys to the extent that felling oak was an offence, other than for the Crown's warships, by the end of the Eighteenth century. As people moved down to the now hospitable valleys, usually along a convenient spring line, the chalk uplands became home to the sheep. Although now bred almost exclusively for meat, it was their wool that made Wiltshire wealthy, probably for the first time since Stonehenge had been built. The barter of wool for the fortified wine – Port - of Portugal is the oldest surviving commercial agreement in the world, but the income it generated was soon mopped up by the rich for themselves. The 1773 Inclosure Act allowed anyone with a title to claim common land as their own, leading to desperate rural poverty. My own home is built on such land, and from the Ridgeway I can see the Lansdowne monument, an obelisk built for the Bowood Estate near Chippenham (just visible down by one of Wiltshire's two River Avons) to mark the end of their land. Bowood has one of Wiltshire's Capability Brown landscapes, although it is less impressive than the garden at Stourhead, down in the south west of the county. Over beyond Chippenham is Malmesbury, home to Dyson and one of the biggest engineering research and development facilities in the country. They also make the odd vacuum cleaner.

Also near Chippenham is Lacock, a village perfectly preserved in time by the National Trust, and the star of many period dramas. I would stay with family here when parents went on holiday, getting soaked in the ford or building model aircraft in the front garden while trying to avoid inquisitive tourists. The village's abbey was confiscated from the church during Henry VIII's reformation and the Fox Talbots who lived there invented photography. It was also used for the first Harry Potter film.

South of Chippenham is Trowbridge where Spitfires were built in the Second World War before being flown to their new bases from a nearby airfield. If I am allowed to wander on the Plain I can see Upavon, where the RAF was born, and beyond that Lark Hill where military aviation first took flight. Above me, as often as not, are the latest military flyers: usually Apache attack helicopters, occasionally a Typhoon.

Up to the north is Swindon where Brunel based his Great Western Railway, now a museum and shopping village. In front of me is Calne, where Harris the pork butchers developed the still famous Wiltshire cure. You still see free range pigs around Stonehenge.

The gentle slope to the west of Devizes is home to perhaps the most impressive run of canal locks in the world. "Putting your back into it" was how a lock was opened, and only the Victorians would think to bring a canal up to a town 400 feet above sea level. It is a mightily impressive sight, and when you get to the top you can visit Wadworth's brewery for a sharpener.

The Ridgeway marks the northern boundary of Salisbury Plain, Europe's largest area of open grassland and the main practice zone for the British army. As reminders of our high tech world Apache attack helicopters are commonplace, fast jets a regular sight and tanks occasionally block the roads. It makes a change from a hunt or a tractor.

So it might look empty, but Wiltshire is home to much of our history. The landscape varies from soaring, open downs to wide, almost empty, valleys. In between are hidden lanes, forests and waterways. Some of it was shaped by man, but much of it remains as it was when man first arrived. I cannot think of anywhere else I would rather live. Give me a year – if only figuratively – to show you its landscape and you will wonder why you just pass through it.

- JANUARY -

EMBRACE THE DARKNESS

A year in the Wiltshire countryside really starts in March, or perhaps late February as the seasons have come to flatten and merge. But that would mean ending this tale in January, and that would be no way to end a book. January is just too bloody miserable. The mornings are not even getting lighter: although the shortest time between sunrise and sunset is usually 21st December, the sunsets will have been getting gradually later for at least a week before that. It can be almost a week into January before sunrise starts to get earlier, and then by just a minute a day. Even by the end of January, while sunset will be almost an hour later than it was just before Christmas, sunrise will be just 26 minutes earlier than its nadir. So it will still be dark for most of us when we've any free time.

Dark out on the countryside of Wiltshire means dark. If it is overcast during the night you will need a torch, ideally where you can reach it if – no, when - there is a power cut. It can be the inky blackness of nightmares, trapped in a madman's cellar. Except you are not trapped at all. You just choose to box set away the evenings because it is dark and cold. And if you do not live in the countryside it is probably not even that dark.

Electric lighting in homes only really got going in the 1930s and, like gas lighting before it, was only available in cities and sometimes the larger towns. Before that, and away from the larger conurbations, candles were the only way of lighting a room after sunset. Despite what you may imagine from the world of period dramas the use of candles was limited. They were expensive. Very expensive in the case of the sweet smelling bees' wax candles seen lighting up an idealised history for many a film or television director. This, perhaps, explains the Wiltshire superstition that it is unlucky to have three lit candles in a room. Most candles were tallow, rendered fat from around the kidneys of livestock. You can guess how they smelt. So most people simply went to bed when it got dark. And disproportionately more babies were born in September as, intriguingly, they still are.

People can also get used to it being dark. The human retina is made up of light sensitive rods and cones, the latter being the most sensitive and adept at distinguishing colour. But the rods are much better at low light levels and, if you give your brain twenty or thirty minutes to adapt, the rods in your eyes can give you a pretty decent black and white view of the night time world.

As to the cold, you'll notice people who live in the country tend to have a collection of coats. Only one of them might be smart, but one will be properly warm and waterproof. It will not have been chosen for its label or looks and it will have been hung next to the dog's coat. It will probably never be replaced, because why would you? If it is warm and waterproof, that is all that matters. It is also true that you can adapt to the cold just as well as the dark. My wife, who grew up in suburbia, cannot believe that I would happily sleep with the bedroom window open all year round. But I always have and, to my father's frustration when we finally had central heating fitted to our home in the Pewsey Vale, I would wake as it heated my bedroom on a winter's morning, and throw open the window. Then go back to sleep, my bedroom on the landing meaning the heat from the sitting room below was also escaping. Yes, I kicked off global warming: sorry about that.

If January's night skies are clear it will be even colder, but far less dark. And Wiltshire will probably be as beautiful as it gets in

January, especially up on the Ridgeway where the blinking lights to the north contrast with the total blackness of Salisbury Plain to the south. Up here the stars really are the stars, the Milky Way a silver smudge from horizon to horizon as you look out from our galaxy. Surely there is nothing more humbling than the realisation there is an infinite universe just sitting there, putting on the greatest show on earth.

The first time I came up here in the dark as an adult was with our son's cub pack. We marched from their base in Urchfont's village hall, up a narrow cutting that the council call Stonepit Lane and everyone else calls dog shit alley. But once you reach the chalk it is practically daylight , even if seven and eight year old boys take great amusement in hiding just long enough to generate anxiety before then rushing out with a loud "BOO!" It is rather more tranquil without them. Alone you can listen for the rustle of a hedgehog, now vanishingly rare, looking for supper among the fallen leaves. Or try to work out where the tawny owls hooting to each other are, the first calling "to-wit", and its potential mate answering "to-woo" back into the night.

If there is no moon the Milky Way might be the most impressive thing in the sky - unless there is a planet in view. In the evenings the planets often show near the western horizon. Jupiter has been impressive this year, a faint red tinge making it easily confused with Mars which, with brilliant Venus, was often called the evening star. Or maybe you would rather spot the constellations named centuries and millennia ago by our forebears and that fascinated me as an Apollo mission obsessed kid. Ursa Major – also called the Great Bear and the Plough – is the easiest to find. Align the two stars at the end of the plough shear and search above them, for about five times the distance between them: that is Polaris, the pole star. Now you have a north point, and can start to put the landscape together. After about 30 minutes you'll find you no longer need a torch.

If there is a full moon it is even easier, although I can get fixated on trying to see the rabbit the Japanese talk of rather than our man in the moon. And the shading of the Sea of Tranquillity where the base of Apollo 11's lunar module still rests. You might think I'm a lunatic for being up here contemplating such stuff in the cold, and therein lies a tale.

The Lunar Society of Birmingham was formed around 1760 by a group of amateur would-be scientists. Its members included Erasmus Darwin, grandfather of Charles, and James Watt, inventor of the steam engine. Joseph Priestley was also a member and would discoverer oxygen when he moved to Calne, lit up brightly to the north of the Ridgeway. People thought they were lunatics because they met on the night of each full moon, but it was simply because it was easier to find your way home when there is a full moon. That is even truer in Wiltshire, with its white chalk paths.

The light of the moon might even be the prosaic explanation for why some people believe planting at full moon gives a better crop. While science has largely dismissed claims as to why it might work – photosynthesis of moonlight and higher water tables, for instance – the practice could have started simply because labourers had no free time during the hours of daylight. In Elizabethan times working hours for labourers were from five in the morning till seven or eight at night from March to September, and from dawn until dusk for the rest of the year. Yes, Sunday was often free but only because the Bible forbade working on the Sabbath, and everybody took the Bible seriously back then.

Staring across Salisbury Plain on a January night, into the dark or up to the stars, it is easy to understand why our forebear believed in hidden hands, gods and spirits. There is no indication it will ever get light again, let alone that the trees will regain their leaves. The wildlife seems to have disappeared and, even to an old agnostic like me, there is something spiritual about this place. If you did not know what most of us have been taught by the time we start secondary education spirits and gods seem as good an explanation as anything. As the constellations nightly circulated the sky people would surely view them as just another cycle of nature.

The countryside is about cycles more than anywhere or anything else. The cycle of the days, the seasons, the years and, ultimately, life. It is hard to believe that I'll bring water up here on a walk in the summer, but the crunch of frost and frozen puddles underfoot in January means that is a way off yet. And watching the planets skate across the sky it occurs to me that atheists, before getting snooty about people who believe the bible is the literal word of God, should remember they probably believe in things that do not actually work – Newton's law of gravity, for example.

You can not see Mercury very often in the night sky, huddled up as it is to the sun, but occasional it is down there, hugging the horizon. Mercury is a mystery, because it does not follow Isaac Newton's laws of gravity. Initially people were convinced there was another planet we had not found to explain the anomaly, but eventually the truth dawned. Mercury is on its own, and our understanding of gravity was flawed. Albert Einstein was the man to work it out: his theory, that what we call gravity is not a force but distortion in space time, is our current best explanation. But, even for space exploration, Newton's gravitational laws work well enough, so Newton's law of gravity is still taught right up until postgraduate level. So we trust in Newton's law, because it works for everything we experience, just as past rituals seemed to work. And as most of the rituals were harmless, would you really avoid them and risk perpetual winter? Failed crops? Coming back from a hunt empty handed? Of course not.

These days Salisbury Plain is home not just home to the myths and legends of our past but also to the most technologically advanced equipment on earth, although using that phrase will come back to haunt me with a dozen paragraphs. This is where our troops have trained for war since at least the nineteenth century, when the war office started buying up the plain. The people of Wiltshire's countryside have often been ridden over in the name of military necessity and occasionally by the desires of the already wealthy yet there is little animosity, just an acceptance that you can not be in charge of everything. Such stoicism is understandable because the two things you notice most in the countryside are two things you have to accept: the weather and the hours of daylight. The comings and goings of the military are small beer by comparison.

Many north Americans have prepared for war here, and the high ground for one group's campsite during World War One in Market Lavington is still known as Canada Rise. Some claimed conditions here were worse than their camp at the Somme, and that is not even the most remarkable thing about the Canadian soldiers' time in Wiltshire. One of them turned up with a pet bear cub that he had to leave behind when he was posted to France. Since the soldier came from Winnipeg the cub was called Winnie, before being despatched to London Zoo. Once there Winnie became a young Christopher Robin's favourite animal and the basis for his father's stories. Yes, Winnie the Pooh lived in Wiltshire with our military, another of their many secrets.

Perhaps our military's love of secrecy is why they love Wiltshire. The red flags and lights ostensibly warn the public it would be foolhardy to enter the Danger Zone (yes, that is how the maps are labelled) and the sounds of shock and awe that often thunder towards us suggest that is the beginning and end of the matter. And yet, a few years ago, when an exercise caused such a huge grass fire the villages below were hidden in smoke for days, the Army refused to allow civilian fire fighters to help. Porton Down, a ministry of defence research facility on the plain, claimed it was simply looking for a cure for the common cold when it was not even on any map available to the public. Locals who worked there suspected chemical weapons research and it was rumoured the entire building could be sent below ground in an emergency, becoming a mausoleum for the unfortunate souls trapped inside. Years ago, visiting nearby premises in pre-satnav days, I was warned that where a map would show woods, instead there would be towering fences, spotlights and watchtowers - but not to worry: it is the map that is wrong. Stonehenge is not the only mystery in these parts.

Colonel Andrew McInerney is my brother in law but, by some measure, that is the least interesting thing about him. He was a Royal Marine and trained on Salisbury Plain, although like everything in the military it is been reduced to initials: SPTA; Salisbury Plain Training Area.

"Darkness is your friend" Andrew confirms, "although you need to know who's supposed to be with you and where they are. It is really quite liberating to head off into the darkness. As Royal Marines, and as commandos, we were forged on Dartmoor, on foot. Tested in the Elan Valley and Brecon Beacons, across beaches in Skye, the icy fjords of the far north of Norway, and in the dense, humid jungles of Asia. So for us Salisbury Plain is more of a benign environment. It is well drained with no lumpy grass. There's not much to bring you down."

The only issue is the lack of cover on Salisbury Plain. If an infra-red flare goes off overhead your opposition might be able to see you moving as if it were broad daylight, if armed with a suitable piece of equipment – which he will be – while you trek on, convinced your invisibility cloak is still in perfect working order. Worse though is there's nowhere to shelter from rain.

"Cold, clear and crisp is invigorating", Andrew avers, with a lift in his voice that tells of fond memories. "Snow falls off you, and wet clothes can be frozen to bash the ice off. Wet stays with you, makes you cold. Drizzle gets down your neck, decays equipment and morale. Even at two or three degrees centigrade it will kill you in the end. Having to get back into cold, wet clothes is miserable. Even worse is wet with temperature variations: say two or three degrees in the daytime followed by minus ten at night. You get wet, then frozen: a miserable cycle. People take boots and gloves off to find bits missing."

Andrew admits he is enjoying reminiscing more than he realised, happy to share more thoughts instead of preparing for an imminent meeting.

"The plain is beautiful. A mass of space in the middle of congested southern England. I've enjoyed drives, rides, tank battles, helicopter insertions, parachute drops and endless yomps across it from side to side and back again. A cold clear January morning with hoar frost on every blade of grass is spectacular, and warms the heart if not the fingers as you try to stay awake on a long sentry duty.

"It is the place too where, during initial training, we first come across our Army counterparts from Royal Military Academy Sandhurst (RMAS - of course). We, a small group of trainee commando officers, join in the mass gathering of Army officer cadets to take part in a defence exercise called 'Busacco Ridge' - named after Wellington's magnificent ridgeline defence battle of the Peninsular War. We walk in to our allotted positions, 'yomping' with 120lbs on our backs, check arcs, choose a reverse slope, consider angles and depth, lay out our plan, de-turf areas and start to dig, and dig, and dig the solid chalk. We raise our heads and wipe sweat from our eyes as coaches and four tonne trucks disgorge the RMAS students clutching packed lunches and blinking from sleep on their journey. We dig. They lay out their position, and stand back as mini diggers come in and prepare their trenches. We dig. And start to hallucinate from exhaustion. At last we near the end of day two of continuous digging, patrolling and sentry duty. At some stage someone tells us to stop, and gather round to watch a demonstration of 'explosive digging'. This seems to be the answer, and something that we wish had discovered a little over 48 hours ago. Much preparation, borehole sinking, explosive inserting and tamping and fuse measuring, splicing and pairing later we gaze hazily at a spider's web of blue and white det. cord sinking into funnel web holes in the turf. We retire to a 'safe' distance and, with a magician's flourish, the engineer triggers the cord."

CRUMP!

"A cloud of dust obscures the area of interest as we surge forward expecting to see a ready made, sharp sided, six feet deep trench prepared for us. When we get to the site there is some blackened grass and an assurance that 'that should loosen it up a bit for you'. Somewhat let down by the marvels of the 'most technologically advanced equipment on earth', we dig. Once ensconced under wriggly tin arches onto which we've had to replace all the soil that we had previously dug out from below them, and once we are sure the turf has been properly re-laid over the spoil to hide us from aerial surveillance, we sort out sentry routines and patrol patterns, and are then faced with the other side of military life: waiting.

"As a soldier, the plain's a place of grassy rolling openness, nothing too steep, interspersed with awkward blocks of forestry. If you try to hide in them, it is rather obvious where you must be. The ground makes it difficult to sneak up on people, particularly when you are on foot, bent under the weight of everything you own, and they have thermal sight equipped tanks that weigh 18 tonnes and travel smoothly on hydrogas suspension and hydrostatic drive across rolling country at upwards of thirty miles an hour. Give them Apache helicopters and troop carrying helicopters to Find, Fix and Finish you and it can be a bruising experience. Royal Marine Commando units regularly go there to undergo Exercise Wessex Warrior, a training battle partly fought in reality and partly in simulation. Almost every vehicle, soldier and aircraft is fitted with

TESEX [tactical effects simulation] kit, which knows where they are, and what they are doing. The resident training battalion provide the opposition [force -'OPFOR']: they know the ground intimately, and have rehearsed repeatedly. Royal Marines commando units have had both notable successes and very public mediocre performances. The successes seem to arise through either the most rigid adherence to the rules, or from the most unconventional and perhaps unrealistic approaches, such as breaking the unit into small raiding teams and operating in an unpredictable feral swarm."

Andrew also taught me perhaps the most useful trick for wandering around in the dark, learned while been searched out by pyrotechnic flares and spotlights on the plain, but just as handy when dog walking. If a bright light appears, be it a car's headlights or a fellow walker with a powerful torch, just close one eye until they've passed. That way your ability to see in the dark is far less compromised as you carry on admiring the stars.

January used to mean snow in Wiltshire, a blanket across a month that can now pass without a frost or even much rain. Only a few decades ago farmers would erect chestnut palings, miles of temporary fencing, to protect roads from snowdrifts. It would also be the farmers who fired up their tractors to clear the roads, working out from the villages and farmsteads until they met the county council's snowploughs. After the infamous winter of 1962-63 people were prepared: when we moved from London to Wiltshire in 1969 my families' elders would speak with bemusement of people who still talked about that winter, but what had been an inconvenience in London had been gradually starving people to death in Wiltshire. A village shop needed (past tense – they are mostly gone) replenishing by its owner visiting a cash and carry store, and was supplemented by visits from vans selling fresh bread and meat. A weekly trip to the nearest market provided fruit and vegetables, plus whatever looked like a bargain. People could not afford to have banks of tinned food standing by "just in case". Today we spend the smallest proportion of our income on food than at any time in modern history. Food used to be a big slice of the household budget, especially for the many war widows. People also ran out of coal and paraffin for heating, and found themselves at the bottom of a very long list when it came to getting the electricity supply reconnected. Country folk pride themselves on being self-sufficient and, by late January 1963, they had been found more than a little wanting. Even as late as the 1990s I visited a house in Coate, a village in the Pewsey Vale, where the upstairs landing and box room were filled with canned food.

It almost happened again over the winter of 1981-82, by which time heavy snow falls had become rare in Wiltshire, and the chestnut palings had been forgotten, partly because farming and rural communities had been gradually hollowed out since the 1960s. At least farmers still had tractors back then, and again became heroes of many communities: even so, some villages remained cut off for several days. How different it would be today, when few farmers own any tractors or other farm machinery. Instead they employ contractors with equipment that costs more than the average footballer's supercar, relying upon huge fields to accommodate them and make a modest profit.

I can remember clearly when I first saw this brave new world. One dark evening, early in 1979, riding a Suzuki 750 from Devizes towards Avebury, just for the hell of it. The road is called the Beckhampton Straight locally, but at speed it is less and less straight as you reach the big roundabout on the A4. Given motorcycle headlights were not up to much back then you relied on memory to an extent only foolish young men would countenance. And suddenly a huge bank of headlights appeared over to the right, far from where I believed the road to be. Lights that could only belong to a huge juggernaut, a truck lost in a field: but they were too widely spaced for that. This was worth a closer look.

It was an enormous, Kermit green, John Deere tractor, bigger than anything I had ever seen, with either a wide seed drill or sprayer behind and a bank of spotlights in front. It was crawling up and down a field parallel to the road, hidden in the dark until it turned towards me. As it passed, its beetle-browed bodywork killed a chunk of farming and the Wiltshire countryside under its glare. Up until then there was no real reason to be afraid of the dark, but suddenly there was.

It turned out to be a bunch of equipment imported from the United States by a younger son of a local farmer. Short of something unpleasant happening to his eldest brother, he realised he would never inherit the family farm, so looked for an alternative way to earn a living doing what he knew and loved. He had spotted that some of Wiltshire's fields were big, especially where their proximity to ancient monuments had minimised subdivision. I had pulled in where the Wansdyke earthworks bisected the road, on the floor of the valley between Roundway and Bishop Cannings' Downs. For some reason, even back then, this area had been kept clear and open for centuries. Like the area around Stonehenge and Avebury, the latter just a few miles to the north, it had probably been like this for thousands of years.

As agriculture came to define Wiltshire, in went the hedges. Villages would be lined with box, a dense evergreen that keeps curious livestock out of your garden. Fields would be between five and twenty five acres: say three to fifteen football pitches. Hedges kept livestock where it was wanted and out of where it was not. Hedges defined where one farm ended and another began. Hedges marked the divide between arable and pastoral farming. It was cheap and could be laid – that is, trained horizontally – to make it pretty impenetrable to livestock.

But as technology and mechanisation crept into farming through the sixties and seventies people were laid off the land. January had been a time when cutting and laying hedges could be work for farmhands who might otherwise have been paid to sit idle. Automation meant there were fewer and fewer potentially idle hands on a January farm, and hedges became seen as a nuisance. Barbed wire fencing was easier to deal with and, while we might see hedgerows as a wildlife sanctuary, back then wildlife was seen as competition for scarce resources.

So came one of the two biggest changes to the Wiltshire countryside of the last fifty years, and possibly the last five hundred: the grubbing up of hedgerows (the other was Dutch elm disease in the early 1970s). The hedges that provided shelter to many birds and acted as snow breaks at this time of year were now in the way of the new supersize machinery. There was some muttering about the legality of ripping up miles of ancient hedgerow but governments knew that farming was in crisis as our appetite for ever cheaper food sat unsated. So grubbing up hedges was accepted just as those huge, and illegal, adverting hoardings in fields next to motorways are ignored. From the beginning it was decided that any advertising would be a dangerous distraction on motorways, but who can deny a farm a little much needed income?

The loss of hedgerows at least means fewer hedgerows to cut. To protect the few birds that remain, it is illegal to cut hedges during April through July. But the nesting season starts earlier than that in a mild winter so, in practice, the end of January is the last time farmers cut their hedges. This also marks the end of the game bird shooting season, to be sure they can recover and breed. As the days grow noticeably longer the cycles of the countryside start to turn just a little faster, even if floodlighting means darkness is not the restriction it once was. Even local churches are now floodlit, with little thought for what effect that might have on moths and bats. There has even been a campaign to have Stonehenge floodlit. Are we really so afraid of the dark?

Spotting that first giant tractor, I had pulled in by the Wansdyke which, like so much of this ancient landscape, is less understood than you might hope. It was almost certainly defensive, possibly to mark and protect the northern boundary of Wessex. Two raised walls – dykes – are either side of a wide track although there is no evidence it was patrolled and was probably built after the Romans left these parts, between 400 and 700AD. It may have just been built to make droving livestock to and from Bristol easier. But it is impressive: maybe it is not as familiar as Hadrian's Wall, yet it is one of the largest linear earthworks in Britain. It is spectacular walking, except when a busy modern road bisects it. Even now parts of the Wansdyke are used to keep sheep or cattle because farms cannot afford to leave land fallow, prehistoric monument or not. It originally ran from the south of Bristol, although little of the original dyke remains in the west of Wiltshire. But from where I stopped you can walk to its eastern end on the edge of Savernake Forest, on the London to Bristol road we now call the A4, just outside Marlborough.

Savernake Forest, to the north east of Salisbury Plain, is even eerier than the open wilds of Wiltshire in January. The risk of breaking an ankle in a burrow or some such means few wander through here at night, but on an overcast and misty winter's day there is a feeling of being alone yet being watched – which the wildlife is certainly doing, wary of expending energy by fleeing but equally aware man is a predator. Just looking at a bird, safe enough in high branches, will often cause it to fly away. This is the time of year you are most likely to spot deer, denied the cover of foliage and having to travel further to find something to eat, often making do with the bark of young trees. They will prefer to freeze to a hedgerow or tree if they see you, reluctant to burn calories in flight unless they believe it utterly necessary. In earlier times man would have shared this caution as bears, wolves and boar prowled the forest, protecting territory. And possibly looking for lunch.

Savernake is the only forest left in private hands in Britain, yet the owners allow free public access to most of it: restrictions only apply to areas being worked by the Forestry Commission, which leases the forest, and to tracks every New Year's Day to prevent them becoming rights of way. 1100 hectares (2750 acres – about 1700 football pitches) of largely deciduous woodland is a lot of forest in southern England, and much of it has been this way for millennia. When the Normans created another woodland south of here they called it the New Forest to distinguish it from Savernake, although no one is certain about Savernake's age. The earliest reference is in a Saxon Charter from King Athelstan in 934AD, then called "Safernoc", but some of the gnarled, pot-bellied old oaks have been dated to earlier than that. Oak would have been the prevalent tree in the ancient forests of Wiltshire, probably interspersed with beech, ash, elm and other deciduous trees. In January they all seem to be stone cold dead, and will remain that way until April at the earliest. No wonder holly and ivy were revered, seeming to live through the winter. But the tree most worshiped was yew, vibrant – and poisonous – even in the depths of January. The Christians adopted the same awe of yew as their pagan predecessors, with yew trees still found in many churchyards and along pilgrim routes, such as the road to Winchester in the south of Wiltshire.

Today Savernake has the odd conifer but the Forestry Commission, which manages the woodland, are gradually removing them from the ancient parts of the forest while growing them commercially on the previously cleared fringes of the estate. To wander through the depths of Savernake is to know what life was like for our predecessors thousands of years ago. Much of England would have been just like this: even Savernake Forest was ten or fifteen fold as big as it is now just a few hundred years ago. One of the theories as to Stonehenge's placement is that it was a rare clearing in lowland forest – which we know to be true – because its thin topsoil and chalk substrate, just like the downs, made it impossible for large trees to colonise. So forests like Savernake would have been where you foraged, hunted and even kept livestock. Today centuries of falling leaves makes the ground feel as if it is a sprung mattress, or a carpet that used up a lot of underlay. I've never known it freeze solid. There are occasional cattle and sheep left by the Forestry Commission to keep the undergrowth down, but overwintering pigs in woods and forests was normal for their earlier keepers. After all, why keep and feed pigs through the fasts and shortages of the winter months when they are perfectly capable of going feral and grubbing up food for themselves? Then, come spring, round them up ready to breed and fatten in another cycle of life.

You might imagine they would get stolen, which was possible, or claimed by the land owner. But the concept of land ownership was alien at the time. When the Normans set out to write to doomsday book they were astounded at this attitude away from feudal lands. People believed the land was a common and shared asset. You could own the crops that grew, but then someone else might graze animals on it when the crop was safely harvested. Even then, crops that were left in a field after harvest – typically turnips and swedes – became common property. They were known as gleanings, as in to glean: we still use the word with a comparable meaning. Things have not changed as much as you might think.

All this might be hard to believe today, unless you consider that we treat the air we breathe in the same way. Nobody in the countryside suggests building a beautiful wall to keep London's polluted air where it is created, happily allowing London to benefit from the winds that disperse pollutants. Is that so different to sharing the land?

By the end of January the evenings are almost useful as sunset moves out past teatime. There might even be the odd snowdrop by the roadside to offer hope that the worst of winter could be over. But there was a bunch of Wiltshire countrymen who might not have welcomed the lighter evenings: Moonrakers. Originally an insult by excise men, added to turnip pickers and swede bashers as labels for the country folk of Wiltshire, it became a moniker of pride.

Just outside the old town walls of Devizes there has long been a large pond called the Crammer. Some say that the name is a corruption of Crane's pond, although I've only ever seen Canada geese, swans and ducks there. Lorna Haycock, in her excellent book *Guide to Devizes*, decides that the name probably comes from the German "kramer", meaning tradesman. German merchants would set up their stalls on the small green next to the pond, close to the town's south gate.

But the Crammer was not only an excellent watering hole for travellers. Its depth and quiet setting just outside a town full of inns also made it an excellent hiding place and staging post. Contraband brandy barrels, on their illicit journey from the coast, could be weighted and hidden during daylight hours when customs officials patrolled known smuggling routes. Then, as darkness returned, the barrels were recovered to continue their journey to cities where there were plenty of buyers who would never question why they were such bargains. And, as with the Lunar Society, travelling under a full moon was the easiest and fleetest way to travel at night.

Except one night some insomniac excise officers came across a band of smugglers trying to recover their booty from the Crammer using large hay rakes. When questioned on their motives a quick thinking smuggler simply pointed at the reflection of the full moon.

"We're raking for the gurt big yellah cheese", he offered. Unbelievable now, the explanation was taken at face value and the smugglers were left alone, branded as lunatics. Soon their supposed betters added "moonrakers" to the raft of insults reserved for the people of Wiltshire's countryside, never suspecting the sense of pride it raised in those prepared to embrace the darkness.

- FEBRUARY -

WOOL FROM WHITE HORSES

The flywheel of Christmas and the New Year has well and truly run down by February, even as Wiltshire starts to tease you that the worst of winter might be over. The flirting starts when the grassy banks by the side of roads and lanes gradually cover with snowdrops, the first obvious wild flowers of the year, and they have been spectacular in recent years. A neighbour who has lived here for over ninety years confirms we've had some of the finest displays she has ever seen. The smaller variety, with its tiny white flowers, opens first, and the double headed bruisers should be out by the end of the month. My wife did not realise they were a wild flower until she moved to Wiltshire almost thirty years ago. Snowdrops love the well-drained greensand that runs through central and south west Wiltshire, allowing them to spread by division and seed. They are also very easy to spread in a garden: when they look like they are dying back cut out a sod of the earth that they are growing in, dig a similar sized hole where you want them and simply drop the sod in it. It is just like cutting and laying thick turf.

One reason snowdrops may be doing so well is the mild winters and the lack of snow. February's weather could once be the worst of the year, as fresh snow added another layer to the frozen January falls. Our snow free winters even tempts some small scale sheep farmers to have their first lambs in February, although it is a gambolling gamble. In theory the earliest born will make the best prices, being the first of the new season's lamb. In practice that does not always happen and, if February returns to her cruel, capricious ways of decades past, you could be in serious trouble. The ewes need feeding if they are to produce milk for their new charges and even in a mild February it is unlikely grass will be growing. That means buying expensive hay, rather than the sugar beet that sheep still pregnant can survive on.

The irony is that young lambs were not originally prized for their meat, but rather for their promise of a lifetime producing wool. Today it might cost more to have a sheep sheared than the fleece will be worth. Even more frustrating is that you might have to pay for next year's shearing before you get paid for this year's fleece. Now it is only the rapid turnaround of a lamb (a sheep under a year old) for meat that keeps sheep farmers going. Waiting until they are between one and two years old (hogget) or older still (mutton) often is not viable. Yet Roy Kyte turned to sheep farming after watching his father slide towards bankruptcy with cattle and poultry.

"If you look at what it costs to run a small poultry farm a dozen eggs would need to be a tenner for the farmer to make a profit" he rues. You might think you pay a premium for free range eggs to ensure their welfare, but they can still be flocks of 16,000 chickens sharing a field and a barn. Yes, they are much happier than their battery farmed counterparts, but they'll probably have had their beaks trimmed to stop them pecking themselves, a classic sign of distress, or attacking other birds. It is not the way people like Roy want to farm. So sheep it is.

Even sheep farming on small scale is tough, and getting tougher. Economies of scale would mean borrowing money to buy more land, yet something you have no control over can wipe you out. It is hard to imagine the effect the 2001 foot and mouth crisis had on the Wiltshire countryside.

"If it hadn't have been for family credits, I'd have gone bust" Roy admits. The memories of disinfected straw across lanes to try and kill it on any passing car's tyres, the footbaths outside back doors and next to gates, the smouldering funeral pyres might be from a while ago, but they still loom large as a warning of how perilous it can be to live off the land.

Still, the hardships are nothing now compared to those of Wiltshire's shepherds even fifty or sixty years ago. They would have needed to create and maintain dew ponds up on the chalk downs to water their flocks, staying up there for lambing or any sickness. Traditionally shepherds were buried with a tuft of wool between their fingers, so that their occasional absence from church on a Sunday would be understood and they could pass into heaven.

The shepherd's huts that were their home were still rusting in farmyards when I was a child, providing perfect dens and hiding places. Simple, corrugated iron shelters, pulled up behind a small Ferguson tractor in a life far removed from their reinvention as fashionable retreats for glampers and David Cameron. Friends can still remember them in use at Adam's Grave, close to Alton Barnes' white horse, in the 1960s. The shepherd told that the nights were bitterly cold –"bloody freezing" is a phrase a six year old remembers - although that was not necessarily seen a as a bad thing. Long periods below freezing sterilised pig sties and sheep pens, as well as breaking down the soil in the ploughed fields ready for sowing in March. It also makes it easier to store food, which is why British sausages are basically raw meat while on the continent they are more typically cured by drying.

There was a time when sheep farmers – as opposed to their shepherds - became fabulously wealthy. By the fifteenth century England was already producing enough cloth for a healthy export trade. For a brief spell in the sixteenth century it was even a legal requirement for all commoners to wear a woollen cap to church to recognise the importance of the industry. However, while by the eighteenth century exporting cloth became the driver of Britain's wealth, the vast majority of it was seized by a fortunate few.

The story revolves around a war that few have heard of but shaped Wiltshire's landscape for centuries. The war of the Spanish succession was, in essence, the British against their usual foes in Spain and France. It was the old story: royal families unable to agree on who owned what, and where they stood in the pecking order. This was what made me hate history at school, because nobody ever wrote about the lives of the ordinary folk, the ones who had to actually create the wealth and fight the wars. So let me start to put that right.

Oak trees had been over felled in England for centuries, as we deforested so much of the countryside, and there were already shortages of oak timber by Elizabethan times. The war of Spanish succession (1701-1714) meant what little was left was needed for warships, so its use for anything else was outlawed. This meant that many older Wiltshire artefacts and buildings used elm, a timber that can be more attractive than oak but with a heartwood far more prone to rot. Still, given it was nicknamed the Wiltshire weed, there was plenty about.

One of the war's British commanders, John Churchill, was made the first Earl of Marlborough by Queen Anne for his efforts. When he subsequently won a battle near the French village of Blenheim she built him Blenheim Palace, which would become the birthplace and home of one of John Churchill's decedents, Winston: yes, that Winston Churchill, our prime minister in World War Two.

And then there was the 1703 Methuen treaty named after negotiator John Methuen, although it was more commonly known as the port wine treaty. The big deal at the time was that it brought Portugal into the war on the British side and gave us access to her ports. But the lasting part of the treaty, possibly the oldest continuous trade agreement in the world, was to permit the sale of English cloth to Portugal free of duty. In return, Portuguese wines imported into Britain would be subject to a third less duty than wines imported from France. Given that Britain was at war with France there was not much French wine to sell, but the British soon developed a taste for the fortified Portuguese wine from Oporto that we simply called port.

A warm country such as Portugal could never have sheep grow the dense fleeces that were possible in England. Equally we were never going to buy enough port to make it an equal partnership. Fortunately for us the Portuguese found gold in their south american colonies and their wealth quickly flowed into British hands.

Unfortunately that wealth was far from fairly distributed. One reason was the 1773 Inclosure Act that looks like untrammelled greed even now. The rich and titled had been helping themselves to common land for centuries, claiming it encouraged efficiency and prevented laziness. The new act allowed that a petition delivered to Parliament by the landowner, tithe holders and a majority of the people affected could be inclosed, denying common rights. They did not even have to enclose (as opposed to inclose) the land with a fence, hedge or whatever: just (typically) say "nobody else is using it and I need it for my sheep." So common land was added to already wealthy landowners' estates, removing the land commoners – most people – relied on for grazing their own livestock and a chance to grow crops to feed their families. Parliament eventually recognised this, requiring claims to be posted on church doors, although it is hard to imagine landowners worrying about illiterate commoners without a vote doing much to end their claims for ever more land. In Wiltshire this would be followed by a second wave of devastation as the war office gradually hoovered up Salisbury Plain from the nineteenth century on.

On the upside, the Inclosures Act is what gives us our wonderful curved roads and wriggling lanes. Landowners would get to an awkward piece of topography or marshy lowland bordered by streams and decide to end their claim there. Take comfort where you can. And there must have been plenty of lamb to eat, a versatile meat with cuts for grilling, roasting and slow cooking. Left over lamb can be minced for rissoles, seasoned with a cinnamon, a spice used in England since the middle ages. It was just unfortunate commoners now had less land to rear sheep on. Inevitably the desperate would occasionally steal a sheep, despite it being punishable by death. In William Hudson's book A Shepherd's Life (inspiration for James Rebanks' similar, much later, title) the author records that, at Salisbury's Spring Assizes in 1830, of the 130 people tried 29 were sentenced to death and five were transported to Australia. Of the other five were sentenced to fourteen years in prison, eleven more sent down for seven years. No-one was found not guilty: the remainder were required to undertake hard labour. Hudson wonders why there is no revolution, just some breaking up of agricultural equipment that will allow the landed gentry to employ ever fewer workers. But, for the most part, the wealthy just carried on convinced of their God given entitlements.

With sheep at pasture on all this freshly acquired grazing land, an army of weavers working from their own homes and a newly wealthy Portuguese clientele, the sheep farmers became very rich indeed, if possibly a little tired of mutton. The irony is that today a fleece is worth less than it costs to shear a sheep and breeds that do not need shearing are looking to be one possible future.

250 years ago, as now, the wealthy liked to boast of their riches, perhaps the most convincing argument for a sudden rash of white horses in eighteenth century Wiltshire. In 1778 Westbury's horse was recut to the design seen today. It is now entirely concreted over, undertaken in 1957 to mark Queen Elizabeth II's coronation, helped no doubt by the new Westbury cement works that was planned a few miles away. The works' 120m (400ft) chimney would become another part of the Wiltshire's landscape until, in another cycle of life, it was demolished in 2016. Standing next to the white horse, nine year old competition winner Lily Sargent pressed the button

that set off the remote explosion and part of Wiltshire's skyline changed forever.

The lack of snow and frosts in recent decades means Wiltshire's famous white horses remain in view all year round. Many have gone because without regular care grass and weeds overrun the bare chalk, but we still had seven in 1998 and now have eight, together with groups dedicated to keeping the horses clear.

The white horses are not just handsome eye catchers, but are carved into excellent walking country, offering a great excuse to get outside and admire Wiltshire from on high. The thin topsoil covering brilliant white chalk, and the steep scarps below the downs, makes creating a white horse an easy way to make a statement. There were once at least thirteen in the county, possibly inspired by the prehistoric Uffington white horse, just over Wiltshire's north east boundary in Oxfordshire. Yet the Uffington white horse is almost an abstract version of a horse, and much longer than any of its successors. Rather than the noble stance of Wiltshire's white horses it seems to be leaping, with a remarkably long tail. It could almost be a fox, but has been called a white horse for at least a thousand years: the abbey at Abingdon referred to Uffington as a "place commonly known as the white horse hill" in the eleventh century.

Why was it done? Appeals to a horse god, or a god associated with horses are the best guesses. From feast pits we know that the early English hunted horses for food, but by the Bronze Age (2000-800BC) they had been domesticated and were pulling carts and chariots. Horses had, by then, started featuring in religion and myth. Was Uffington really the inspiration for the much later and very different white horses of Wiltshire? There is an intriguing possibility that it is.

The oldest white horse in Wiltshire is the one furthest from Uffington, thirty miles to the south west, between Bratton and

Westbury. It is also very different to the one at Uffington, a noble beast standing aloof with no sense of movement. Like all the old Wiltshire white horses it faces to the left, where Uffington's flies to the right. Cut just before 1700, the most intriguing thing about the Westbury white horse is that it was said to be cut to obliterate an earlier, much smaller white horse described as a "grotesque creature". This predecessor has been said to represent King Alfred's charger Swallow, which he rode to victory over the Danes at the nearby battle of Ethandune in 878, although this is controversial.

Research in the 1880s by the wonderfully named Reverend Plenderleath suggests it was a "dachshund-like animal, with long heavy body", and a crescent at the end of its tail as well as a decorated saddlecloth. He became convinced it was a contemporary of the Uffington horse, and that many of the Wiltshire white horses replaced earlier chalk figures that formed a ring around Avebury. It is an intriguing theory that is respected despite no excavations of the current white horses to see if there is any evidence left. In Plenderleath's 1892 book, *The White Horses of the West of England*, he includes an illustration by "Gould, editor of Camden" that does bear a resemblance to the horse at Uffington.

The current Westbury white horse is cut onto an incredible 50 degree steep scarp, well over twice as steep as any of the world's steepest roads. It stands below an Iron Age (900BC-100AD) hillfort known as at Bratton Camp. Here, high above the ancient forests in the valley below, there were round houses, granaries, stores and workshops. The people who lived here wore clothes of woven cloth and owned jewellery, probably from overseas. Their circular houses with thatched roofs were set around a communal, paved area. They ate from bowls and plates, in a way of life we would recognise. But these were violent times, and they would have needed their bronze swords and daggers. Bratton Camp was an easily defended home to the peers of the Uffington white horse's creators: there is no reason to suppose they would not want their own white horse.

Plenderleath writes that the old Bratton Camp white horse was destroyed "in 1778 by a wretch by the name of Gee, who was steward to Lord Abingdon." What intrigued him is that the new horse could have been more easily cut if it faced right, as the old horse did. Instead it faces left, as do all the old Wiltshire white horses. Why? Plenderleath's book always uses the heraldic practice of describing things as facing the way a knight would describe the design on his shield – as he holds it, rather than as it is seen by others. So the original Bratton Camp horse faced sinister (right to an observer, left if you were behind it) and the new one "dexter". Could it have been a Christian sensibility? We will probably never know.

Theories as to why Lord Abingdon cut the new horse include showing allegiance to the House of Hanover, which used a white horse as a heraldic symbol. Or it might be as simple as "because I can". Follies – buildings with no obvious purpose – were becoming fashionable, initially in gardens and later as eye catchers, often miles away from their owners' house. The steep scarp was pretty much worthless since the only use for these downs was grazing sheep – not goats - for their wool. It is also true that farmhands were always found work even when there was little to do: extending the estate's stone walling and now, perhaps, creating a white horse. But the truth is we do not know, even though it is just a few hundred years ago. All the locals can tell you is that when the nearby Bratton church clock strikes midnight, the white horse goes down to the Bridewell Springs to drink. Similar legends come with other white horses.

After Westbury white horse's 1778 update the copycats came in a rush. By 1780 the Cherhill horse had been cut on the outskirts of the Bowood Estate, just below the Lansdowne monument which was built in 1845 by the third Marquis of Lansdowne, allowing him to point out where his estate then ended. You cannot help but suspect the same motive for the white horse.

Like the Westbury white horse, the one at Cherhill stands below prehistoric earthworks, in this case Oldbury Castle. The horse was the work of Christopher Alsop of Calne, known locally as "the mad doctor". It is claimed he had the horse cut out while shouting instructions from a megaphone. Alsop knew the famous horse portraitist George Stubbs which may explain his motive. The white horse overlooks Labour-in-Vain Hill which I always imagined referred to its apparently deceptively shallow but exhausting climb over several miles to Avebury. Even so, the nearby Labour-in-Vain pub had, until quite recently, a hanging sign illustrated with a nursemaid trying to scrub a black boy clean. How times change.

The next white horse was not far away. It was cut in 1785 at the eastern end of the Pewsey Vale, for Robert Pile of Manor Farm in Alton Barnes, several miles to the west: Pile would not have been able to see it. Alton Barnes gained its own white horse in 1812, again paid for by one Robert Pile although, given the passage of time, it might have been his successor rather than the same person. The Alton Barnes horse is still in magnificent order and has been regularly "scoured", that is to say weeded and topped up with fresh chalk. The sight of army helicopters with slings of fresh chalk below was something many of us found magnificent entertainment. Milk Hill, just above Alton Barnes, is Wiltshire's highest point, so this is perhaps the finest of the white horses. It is also next to the valley where the most famous of Wiltshire's many crop circles was created, the one featured on Led Zeppelin's 1990 "Remasters" compilation album, but that is for a much later chapter.

The Pewsey horse was refurbished in 1789 but the landowner was so appalled by the revelries of the scourers that he refused to allow it to happen again. Inevitably the cutting disappeared but, in 1937, a Mr George Marples was in the area researching the old white horse. He persuaded locals looking to commemorate George VI's coronation that a new white horse, close to the site of the old one, would be the perfect celebration. Although smaller, less well maintained, and more hidden away than some other surviving white horses it is worth seeking out. Not only is it surrounded, as all the white horses are, by some wonderful walking countryside the pubs of Pewsey are in easy reach.

Another small white horse that needs seeking out is the one at Marlborough, cut by the pupils of a local school in 1804. The school is long gone, but the famous Marlborough college, which the then Kate Middleton attended, includes a reference to it in the college's song:

And when to Marlborough old and worn we shall creep back like ghosts

and see youngsters yet unborn run in between the posts,

ah, then we'll cry thank God, my lads, the Kennett's running still,

and see the old White Horse still pads up there on Granham Hill.

Convention now has the river Kennet spelt with one t, even if the West Kennett it flows through has two. These inconsistencies abound in Wiltshire and, surely, elsewhere.

A few miles north of Marlborough, just below the Ridgeway, is the Hackpen white horse. Again, there are many prehistoric earthworks nearby including the hillfort at Banbury Castle which gives its names to a local event for real horses, the Banbury International Horse Trials.

Hackpen's white horse is a rather modest affair, not helped by the shallow slope it occupies. It is also known as the Broad Hinton white horse because it is thought to have been cut for that village's parish clerk, Henry Eatwell, in 1838 to salute the coronation of Queen Victoria.

Just to the west of Broad Hinton, cut into a fabulous scarp is the Broad Town white horse, small but perfectly formed. All that can be traced of its origin is another note by Reverend Plenderleath from 1885. In it he dates the horse to 1864 and credits a local farmer, William Simmonds, with its creation.

And then the fashion for white horses seems to have died, as quickly as it had begun. The only revival of interest in cutting chalk figures came during World War One, when soldiers from Fovant camp carved a badge into the downs west of Salisbury. The first is claimed to have been cut by the City of London Rifles in 1916, and there are still eight remaining military insignia cut across the Cranbourne Chase and West Wiltshire Downs, the last created in the 1970s. However, another twelve have been lost through lack of scouring, just as with the white horses.

There were at least another five white horses in Wiltshire that are known to have existed and they were all cut in the nineteenth century. Many were so short lived they never made an Ordnance survey map. The lost white horse that fascinates me most is the one on Tan Hill, just above the village of All Cannings where I grew up. It is near the site of what was a huge livestock market, which had been held for hundreds if not thousands of years. There are records that it was first cancelled in 1637 to prevent the spread of the plague and again in 1914 when the gold standard was dropped during the war and farmers could draw no cash. Otherwise it ran continuously as a market and public holiday until 1932. It is not known when it started but sheep have been kept in the area for at least 2500 years.

The Tan Hill horse was first recorded in Kathleen Wiltshire's surprise 1975 literary hit *Wiltshire Folklore*, a follow up to her *Ghosts and Legends of the Wiltshire Countryside*. Mrs Wiltshire was a legend in the village, an elderly widow living alone in a terraced thatched cottage next to the churchyard. Mothers would warn us to stay away muttering, when pressed, that she was a witch. This was catnip to young boys, who would try to lure her outside to get a better idea of what a witch might look like, or could tell us. Once overhearing us loudly deciding to drink from the church's font she rushed out with a jug of orange squash, making us swear we would never drink holy water, which of course we had no intention of doing. We just wanted to pester her for stories. I've largely forgotten her horrible histories but remember a friend blurting out, "my mum says you're a witch". To our astonishment she smiled, stooped even lower, and whispered "But a white [good] one, dear, so you're alright."

As I became a teenager inevitably other interests took over and, as other outsiders of whom my family had been the first moved in, her powers seemed to wane. And then she was persuaded to tell her stories for publication and she became famous – rather than infamous, I suppose – in the village once more. Suddenly she was telling her stories at WI meetings and dropped claims of having been involved in witchcraft: rather she was just a keeper of old myths and stories.

One of her tales involved a long lost "white donkey, its head too big to be a horse" up on Tan Hill, close to a stone circle. On our many expeditions up there we found nothing, but hunted on in the hope of securing our very own Stonehenge. Within the past twenty years more determined people have discovered partial remains of both the stone circle and the donkey, but little is left of either. The 1890s Ordnance Survey map actually records the stone circle, although no white horse, and tells that Tan Hill was then Saint Ann's Hill. A quick tour of the internet reveals the Catholic Church's belief that Saint Anne (with an e) was married to a shepherd from Bethlehem, so perhaps there is a tenuous connection. Saint Anne's day is July 26, and the fair was held in early August so there is possibility it was on the first Saturday after the saint's day. Or could it just be Christianity absorbing older traditions again? Others claim that tan is the Celtic word for fire and the Romans called the place Tan Fauna: the place of fire animals, or a feast place.

The Tan Hill sheep market died during the Great Depression and, like every Wiltshire village I know, the young men it needed most were lost in Europe's terrible wars, their names on the memorial next to Mrs Wiltshire's house. Or perhaps we had started to rely on motor vehicles and Tan Hill was difficult to get to compared to the markets in Devizes, Marlborough and Pewsey.

In my time the farm at Cannings Cross was arable, growing wheat and barley where once sheep had grazed on the lower slopes of the downs below the chalk. But well researched excavations established that sheep were farmed here as far back as 650BC, along with cattle, goats and pigs. There were still a few sheep here in the 1970s, although probably less than there are now. The changes came quickly, certainly within a generation, after thousands of years of sheep on the downs being the accepted order of things. Joining the "Common Market", as it was back then, did not help because our low volume, high welfare, farming practices could not compete with the continent's intensive farming methods, especially for pigs.

One farmer who is entirely unsentimental about these changes is Chris Combe, whose family has farmed in the shadow of Roundway Hill and Oliver's Castle since 1970. Most of his 300 hectares (about 725 acres) has always been arable but, as well as his late father's prized pedigree Hereford cattle which brought little income but huge pride, pigs were also viable to start with. Today all the stalls have been converted or rebuilt as offices, workshops and even a yoga studio. Chris is adamant that farming must rely upon good management rather than subsidy and sentimentality, and that if pigs are not profitable, but letting out their converted sties is, heritage has to take a back seat.

"There were 850,000 sows in this country when I left university, but there are now only about 400,000. It's not that we're eating less, but that we import more. But then we don't grow oranges or bananas in this country and I eat them every week. We need to get across to consumers that, along with Sweden, our welfare standards are the highest in the world. Half the pigs in this country are outside [effectively free range with shelters] or in open barns. They all have straw bedding. You just cannot compare our animal welfare with somewhere like Belgium. Consumers can know that if they buy British pork the little bit extra they pay has given that animal a far better life than if it was reared anywhere else."

Chris has a very good point. People often comment on all the happy pigs rooting about in the fields to the south of Stonehenge. It must be a welcome relief from the traffic jams that are the norm on that part of the A303. Compare that to thousands of miles I have travelled in Italy, a country renowned for its produce, yet I've never seen a pig there. I spent a week riding over a thousand miles around Sicily, feasting on pork products, without seeing a solitary porker. The reason I was given is that pigs can get sunburnt, which is true. And is why pigs always have field shelters in Wiltshire.

Before leaving Chris's farm there is another white horse to admire close to hand, one carved in 1999 to celebrate the millennium. Chris allowed part of his land to be used, even though "bloody bureaucrats decided to dock me £37 a year for it." Chris considers it a crying shame that a steeper slope for it could not be found, because the area is full of protected landscape. But it is only really slightly disappointing from Chris's farm: driving to visit him you come down the Devizes link road to see the horse perfectly. Even better is from the Ridgeway where it makes a fantastic addition to Oliver's Castle, which is where people originally wanted it. From many other places you can see it at the same time as the Alton Barnes' white horse, apparently running towards its older stablemate.

The suggestion for the new white horse came from an incomer, as new things often do in Wiltshire. People were originally wary of new blood since, too often, newcomers did not want to get involved with the community. I moved here too young to realise that in cities, and increasingly towns, people consider it good form to keep yourself to yourself. Out here the opposite is the case. Working as a shepherd could mean days or even weeks of isolation, seeing nobody but the young lad who brought sandwiches up from the village, so company is welcomed, albeit with great subtlety. It also creates a certain taciturn nature. In the 1980s I was frustrated at being unable to find a house where I had an appointment with the owner, running late because I thought I knew the area well and should have had no trouble finding my way. Relieved to find the obligatory old boy leaning against a gate in the middle of nowhere I asked if he knew the address.

"What name?" he asked. Addresses are, of course, only for the convenience of postmen. I told him.

"Wouldn't start from here if I were you", was his pensive reply. "Go back the way you just came." So I did. And yes, I was late for my appointment.

At least I could understand my guide. Although there is a definite Wiltshire accent, deeper and formed further back in the mouth than the Somerset burr, as a kid it could sometimes seem impenetrable, to me at least. I remember leaning against another gate at least twenty years earlier when a friend asked his father for an opinion on whether some new farming practice was better than the old way.

"Cassent see it, snow" he offered, and wandered off. Apparently he could not see it himself, but you never know…

In 2016 a survey of 4000 people made headlines by claiming that only a half of us know their neighbours' names and a third do not meet with friends or family regularly. In the Wiltshire countryside people not only know their neighbours' names, but also their neighbours' neighbours' names, along with a raft of information about them going back decades. Incomers sometimes find this hard to come to terms with. Others embrace it as a liberating call to arms.

As Sarah Padwick did, newly arrived in the area in 1998, writing to the Devizes Gazette and Herald newspaper to suggest that a hill figure be cut on Roundway Down to celebrate the millennium.

Unknown to Sarah, there had been moves many years before to restore Devizes' original white horse, first spotted in 1954 by a young cyclist, the remains of its outline revealed by a light dusting of snow. Since the cyclist, James Smith, was head boy of the local grammar school he was the sort of chap able to encourage others to join him in researching the subject, which they did.

Although no drawing of the white horse could be found, there was plenty to discover. The horse had been cut in 1854, paid for by local shoemakers and known as snobs' horse. Snob was the old English word for shoemaker, which gained its current meaning because shoemakers' were seen as people constantly looking up to, and trying to please, their supposed betters. Eventually the original snobs tired of this and returned to calling themselves shoemakers. Equally sadly snobs' horse became as unloved as its prefix and, by 1922, had disappeared.

But once people knew it was there it was noticed again and again. Under certain lighting or weather conditions a picture was built up of its original outline. Assuming it had been built the usually way, with a trench forming the outline followed by scrapping away the topsoil inside the outline, restoration would surely be possible. Yet the scarp was by then designated an SSSI (site of special scientific interest) and government agencies threw up the usual figurative hands of horror that will probably make sure the A303 by Stonehenge is never upgraded.

Instead, armed with knowledge of the original outline it was decided to cut a new white horse on the other side of Roundway Hill, reversed so that, uniquely of Wiltshire's white horses, it faces right looking across the Pewsey vale to its compatriot at Alton Barnes.

By 1999 it was ready for the millennium and has been regularly scoured by groups that have included the residents of the nearby Erlestoke prison. While I am chatting to Chris Combe he asides that the Scouts are up their now, keeping it pristine. Wiltshire might be losing its income from wool, but at least it is gaining white horses.

- MARCH -

THINGS CAN ONLY GET BETTER

By the beginning of March the fields are greening up with the winter wheat and barley, perhaps even lighting up yellow as the oil seed rape comes into flower. There will still be bare edges to the fields, and scraps of land left unused, usually to claim one of the many subsidies available to farmers. The difference between making sure all these are applied for and claimed can be the difference between survival and bankruptcy for a farm. Yet you only need a few acres to be able to claim, so some people are effectively getting paid to have a nice garden just because it is not producing any food: they might also get paid to add some hedges. Even more difficult to understand is that it is claimed that ninety per cent of subsidies are going to ten per cent of farmers. And they are often not even what most of us would call farmers: one of the biggest beneficiaries in recent years has been the Emir of Dubai, paid over £600,000 in a single year for what most of us would consider to be a private stable of race horses.

Another of the biggest claims, which total over £3 billion a year, has been by Sir James Dyson, who made his fortune at his research and manufacturing facility near Malmesbury in north west Wiltshire. This is hardly what the public imagines their taxes are being spent on when government talks about looking after farmers. The fact that these subsidies originate in the European Union's rule book meant people were surprised when many farmers voted leave in the 2015 referendum. When you see who actually gets the money, it makes more sense.

Instead you might think that we should not be subsidising businesses that employ less than two percent of the population while generating less than a tenth of gross domestic product (the money Britain generates). You might be surprised to find arable farmer Chris Combe agrees with you.

“Farming did OK for a few thousand years without subsidies. The difference between say the top 25 per cent of farms who are successful and the bottom 10 per cent is good management and innovation. The average age of a British farmer is 59, a lot of them just clinging on thanks to subsidies and not prepared to change their ways. Their kids won’t want to take over the farm, so they’re just putting off the inevitable. If they sell up the land will be hoovered up by farms with good management and the vacuum gets filled. And if some land just gets forgotten and overgrown with brambles, well, people can either leave it or clear it if they’re bothered about it.”

Or those scraps of land can be left for wildlife. Wandering by Wiltshire’s monster fields the lack of diversity is alarming. Until you get onto the MoD’s part of the plain there is little birdlife, even though it should be starting to appear in March. Get onto the Salisbury Plain training area, or down by the hedgerows and there are now plenty of birds. That is not so in the big arable fields, where even the weeds do not grow, although that might be changing.

“Milder winters mean we can plant in the autumn”, Chris confirms “so when the weather warms up the crops get a head start compared to spring planting. But some weeds are starting to develop resistance [to sprayed pesticides] so maybe we will go back to spring planting.”

In 2017 the talk was of a dry winter and a lack of rain. This has an impact on arable farmers and pastoral (livestock) farmers alike, because it is needed to make crops and grass grow. But in recent years the concern has been too much rain, and the flooding it brings. Wiltshire's chalk downlands do not absorb huge quantities of rain, but rather direct it to the valleys below. Our problems are really nothing compared to Somerset or the Lake District, but the frustration directed at London is felt as keenly. During this century our government plans to spend £3.7 billion on flood defences, almost as much as is spent of farm subsidies every year. And, according to the BBC, almost half of that will be spent to the benefit of London and the surrounding area. This is the same BBC that did not report on West Country's 2014 floods until they reached then prime minister David Cameron's Oxfordshire constituency. As one farmer put it to me, after floods had ruined his crops, "we need to take down the Embankment and Thames barrier and then see how Westminster feels about flood defences."

Londoners may believe that they get first dibs on all infrastructure spending because they generate so much of Britain's wealth. But think about that: arguing that the rest of the country is not deserving of investment because it does not generate wealth. That can be extended to an argument in favour of abolishing taxation and the state. And where do city dwellers think their food comes from, their pollution is dispersed and their water comes from? It is a very symbiotic relationship.

There is some hypocrisy here when, as a nation that was once almost entirely forest, we complain about deforestation in South America and, as my would be guide in the last chapter put it, "I wouldn't start from here if I were you". But here is where we are, relying on farmland and valleys that flood partly because of that deforestation. The flooding also starts along our roads and villages because roads, driveways and such literally pool and direct the water.

It is not even that the 2014 floods on Salisbury Plain were especially bad. Tilshead is often called the village at the centre of the plain and, in just a few hours on Saturday January 16, 1841, nine houses were destroyed. Lives were saved by smashing roofs or clinging to a chimney. Nearby villages lost another half dozen or so houses. There is no river here to carry water away, so it just collects until it can seep into the waterlogged greensand.

The issue was not just that so much rain ran off the downs above, but also that the traditional building material here is cob. Little more than mud and straw, covered with a lime render, it was no match for a metre deep, ten mile an hour, tidal wave that even horses could not fight. Drainage is much better now, rebuilding and improvement helped by a national appeal that followed, but it is a warning that we fail to invest at our peril.

The costs of recent flooding included the emergency services dealing with flooded houses, weeks of diverted traffic from one of Wiltshire's main roads, the council dealing with the aftermath, including completely relaying large sections of the roads. Then there will be the insurance companies' loses, and this is just the money side of flooding. The human misery, the loss of mementoes and heirlooms, children missing school, are all things that are gone forever. And while the loss of crops is obvious, flooding can also reduce the quality of the soil, affecting future harvests.

Flooding can, however, be beneficial for farming if carefully managed. Water meadows, man made features that can date back 400 years, take advantage of adjoining watercourses, extending the growing season by controlled flooding. Because river water is usually above the five degrees centigrade that grass needs to grow you can graze animals and plant wheat earlier than would otherwise be possible. Now they are valuable as a wildlife habitat, although few have survived the expansion of our towns and cities and the intensification of framing.

Yet right next to Salisbury is one of the finest surviving water meadows in the world. Harnham water meadow was subject to inclosure in 1787 but its earliest mention was in 1669, when British agriculturalist John Worlidge wrote in his treatise of English farming, *Systema Agriculturae*, that water meadows were "one of the most universal and advantageous improvements in England within these few years."

Although sheep are hardy enough to be left on Wiltshire's downs all year round the grass they feed on will not grow unless temperatures rise above three to five degrees centigrade. Historically, then, that meant feeding the sheep for weeks, if not months, during the winter, typically with hay cut and dried in early summer. But even with a great harvest you need somewhere to keep the hay dry for potentially ten long months.

River water, however, rarely gets as cold as five degrees centigrade. By diverting river water onto adjoining fields, known as floating, water meadows were created. Grass could be persuaded to grow much earlier than it did up on the downs, potentially by several weeks. Subsequent filling of the irrigation channels was known as drowning, the idea being to warm the soil, and gain valuable nutrients from Wiltshire's fast moving, chalk bedded, rivers and streams. The aim was to move the water "on at a trot and off at a gallop".

During the eighteenth century, alongside the huge increase in wool production, the harvest of wheat and barley rose just as dramatically in Wiltshire. A report in 1794 claimed that the "first reason to keep sheep was for their dung and the second the wool". The Wiltshire Longhorns were apparently happy to make their way from the downs to the water meadows at the end of each day, and equally happy to stay in a closely huddled flock at night where they would unwittingly fertilise the water meadows, ready for them to be sown with corn. This being the case the irrigation channels must have run much further into Wiltshire's lowlands than they do today. Even so, a walk along the River Avon, especially as it travels to and from Salisbury, is to find not only water meadows but trout farms and other uses of its waters.

You will also get to share some of the views of Salisbury Cathedral that so bewitched John Constable. Hopefully plans to reinstate a vista he painted in 1825 will reappear sooner rather than later, as the cathedral school wants to open up its grounds and relocate a works yard. It is not coincidence that the cathedral was built by the river either. Rivers were the easiest way to move building materials, and much of the cathedral is Tisbury stone from a quarry by the River Nadder that feeds the water meadows. The Chilmark quarry is closer still, and the Purbeck stone would have come up the river Avon that flows though the water meadow, absorbing the Nadder as it does.

That the cathedral did not collapse built on such waterlogged land has been attributed to the speed at which it was built. While most cathedrals took over a century to build, Salisbury's was consecrated 38 years and five months after its foundation stone was laid on April 28, 1220. Over the next 46 years it gained extensions and improvements, all apart from the bell tower still on show. The cathedral's greatest triumph, the spire, rose up between 1300 and 1320, taking its place as one of the most recognisable features of the Wiltshire landscape. Although the pre-great fire of London's St Paul's and Lincoln cathedrals both had taller spires their timber and lead pointers are long gone, and since the late sixteenth century Salisbury's stone clad call to pilgrims has been tallest in England, at 123m (404 feet). Yet my favourite part of the cathedral must be the cloisters, a sanctuary for peaceful refection as much now as when it was built.

Salisbury Cathedral is still very much a living part of modern Christianity, but elsewhere in Wiltshire is another cloister by another River Avon that has a very different history. Lacock Abbey's foundation stone was laid on April 16, 1232, next to the River Avon that rises far to the north in South Gloucestershire, before flowing through Wiltshire and on to the Bristol Channel. Salisbury's Avon originates in the Pewsey Vale, joining the River Stour on its journey south to the English Channel. That there is more than one River Avon is simply explained: avon is from an old Celtic word for river; yes, it is the River River.

Lacock Abbey's first Augustinian nuns would have had, for the time, a comfortable life on the profits of wool, their sheep thriving on the rich surrounding farmland. There was also the adjoining village for their workers and an impressive tithe barn where local farmers were expected to leave a tenth of their crop for the benefit of the church. What could possibly go wrong? Ah, that would be Henry VIII's taste for wives and arguments with Rome.

The dissolution of the monasteries between 1536 and 1541 was Henry's fearless looting of monasteries and convents, and an abbey is a monastery or convent attached to a church. Selling Lacock Abbey to Sir William Sharington netted Henry £783, and ensured the church was demolished. Since then the abbey has been a private house, albeit today with good access afforded by the National Trust. You can visit the room where the inventor of photography, William Henry Fox Talbot, created the earliest surviving negative in 1835, taken of a small window.

The cloisters that adjoin the house are now most famous for their role in *Harry Potter and the Philosopher's Stone*, the first of the film franchise. You can even sit in the room where spells were taught, with its 500 year old warming pot. But the setting was generally ruined by the secrecy the movie makers demanded, with the abbey grounds fenced and the lower stories of the abbey boarded over. Thankfully they have never returned.

You can wander around Lacock spotting where other dramas have been filmed, but the best walk is the one along the river from the abbey to Bewley Common, where there is a fine old stone bridge to match the causeway at Lacock. This was where I would fish for perch, with my father casting for something bigger that we could take back to the table. Kingfishers and herons are too aloof to care if you spot them and, by the end of March, the wild garlic might have started to show. Climbing up Bowden Hill is hard work but can be rewarded with one of the finest bluebell displays in the country, never mind the county. And because this really is a hill, rather than the beginning of another down, the views are magnificent in every direction. From up here you can spot Melksham – thought to mean milk and ham, although ham once also meant village. Just beyond is Trowbridge – a bridge over the River Biss, the reason for Trow unknown. Both these towns were involved in Spitfire production during the war. A little further away is Bradford-on-Avon (a broad ford across the Avon), where Royal Enfield built their later motorcycles in a disused Bath stone quarry. Shifting production here made the factory less vulnerable to German bombers than Enfield's original home in Redditch, south of Birmingham and Coventry.

Another wonderful aspect of being in open countryside is that you are aware of the wind's direction, and able to learn what this means. In built up places, even in narrow valleys, the wind is just blowing whichever way it can, constrained by topography. Out in the open it shows its true self. From the south west comes the gulf stream, and potentially rain. Or warm, settled weather: it is a lottery. From the north west squally rain is almost certain, but a north easterly rarely brings rain, just icy blasts. Changes are also noticeable and, as wind direction veers – moves clockwise – or backs anticlockwise, you can decide whether to stop for a picnic or scurry back to the car.

As March moves on the early leaves start to appear, and the first growths and goose grass ("sticky willy", as my wife calls it) from the hedgerow would have once been harvested. After a long winter with no fresh greenery to eat these were a valuable source of vitamin C, something our seafarers had discovered the need for the hard way. The British are known as limeys simply because our ships carried so many limes, to protect their crews from scurvy. Wiltshire country folk ate greenery – including wilted or boiled young nettles for the same reason. Hawthorn's early growth was prized enough to be nicknamed bread and cheese, and others were a vital feed for livestock being driven to market. Anywhere called goose green or goose hill is likely to have been first recorded as a staging post on a long drove.

We also cross the spring (vernal) equinox around the 21st of the month, which will be celebrated at Avebury and especially Stonehenge, if not on the scale reserved for the summer solstice. The mad march hares will now be running about, their blood rising as the mating season is upon us. The days are finally longer than the nights.

Hares are magnificent creatures that, like so much of our wildlife, have suffered from a combination of intensive farming and, in Wiltshire at least, our obsession with protecting the badger. Badgers no longer have any natural predators in Britain, and feast upon leverets – baby hares – nesting in open countryside. They are also driving hedgehogs to extinction here: I think it must be 15 years since I last saw one. Ditto frogs and ground nesting birds. It feels wrong to protect one species to the detriment of so many others.

Hares are beautiful creatures on open grassland and are Britain's fastest runner, able to flee at the thick end of 50mph. Their leverets are born ready to run in nests on the grassland they call home, unlike the blind rabbit kittens which rely on the protection of a burrow. By March hares' ritual dances makes the countryside look to be hosting a boxing tournament. Occasionally they will leap up for no apparent reason, perhaps to see further afield or attract a mate, and it is well worth watching out for as a harbinger of spring.

The hare is also our "Easter bunny". Nesting among birds such as the skylark and corn bunting, people would see hares flee and assume the birds' nests and eggs were the hares', not realising the leverets had gone into hiding. The eggs would be collected and decorated, with a celebration on the equinox that may have celebrated a fertility goddess Eostre – Easter. Like so many other apparently Christian celebrations Easter was hijacked from earlier beliefs. Hardly an unreasonable practice given that few are going to convert if they have to give up all their old revelries. But now, rather than being fixed, Easter is the first Sunday after the first full moon on or after the equinox, tying it the Jewish Passover that took place just before the resurrection of Christ.

Ironically the National Trust was chastised in 2017 for holding "Cadbury creme egg hunts" causing our permanently outraged press to demand the word Easter was inserted between "creme" and "egg", ignoring the likelihood this was a matter of sponsorship, and that Easter was mentioned elsewhere on posters and advertisements. Editors railed that "Easter egg hunts" were a Christian tradition and should be always be recognised as such. In fact they probably pre-date Christianity.

The greatest Easter tradition in Wiltshire is the Devizes to Westminster canoe race, the toughest event of its type in the world. The two seater craft set out along the Kennet and Avon canal, eventually joining the River Thames. This is where the skill is, timing the race on the still waters of the canal to catch the turning tide at Teddington that will help you on your way to Westminster. The main class faces a non-stop 125 miles of rowing and, despite some elite entrants over the years, the official record set in 1979 still stands.

Wiltshire's long connection with the military is what set the "DW" on its road to fame. Members of the SAS, Paratroopers and Royal Marines saw it as a fine proving ground for their special talents and reserves of endurance. Initially the race required entrants to be entirely self-sufficient but eventually it was realised this favoured the armed forces and the requirement was dropped in 1971. Eight years later civilians set what is still the official course record of

15 hours 34 minutes, benchmarked by Brian Greenham and Tim Cornish.

The event traces its roots to 1920, when national rail and bus strikes seemed inevitable. In a Pewsey pub a bet was on: could a crew get down the River Avon from Pewsey to the sea at Christchurch in under three days, a distance of some 70 miles. The answer was yes, easily. Further wagers and records followed.

In 1947 one of the original four canoeists, Roy Cooke, decided on a new challenge, attempting to row to London via the derelict Kennet and Avon canal and the River Thames in less than 100 hours. He failed, but the following year Devizes Scouts were promised money from various sources – they were all 17 so there could be no betting involved - if they could take "a boat from Devizes to Westminster in under 100 hours, all food and camping kit to be carried in the boats".

Devizes Scouts are one of the oldest Scout troops in the world, established in June 1908 by Lieutenant Colonel Kenneth Steele, a brother-in-arms of founder Lord Baden-Powell. Thus started a long association between the military and scouts competing in the DW. In the first true race Scouts Peter Brown, Laurie Jones, Brian Smith and Brian Walters completed the journey in 89 hours 50 minutes. The DW was on.

The race started, as it still does, at the old wharf a few yards upstream of the final of the 29 locks that mark the climb to Devizes, all long derelict by the time of the first DW. I spent many miserable hours in them as a teenager, helping to clear them as part of my Duke of Edinburgh's award community service. They had become a dumping ground and mosquito swamp, and memories of hauling a huge pink mattress out still haunts me. But beyond here the canal still held water, albeit thickly coated with duckweed sown onto its surface during the war to prevent German bombers using it to pick out their way to Bath and Bristol. This is why the DW was always held over the Easter weekend, before the duckweed built up to a thick growth during the spring and summer, eventually choking the life out of it and leaving a trail of upended and very dead fish. Looking at the waterway now, with narrow boats and restored locks, is much more pleasing.

Setting a fast time in the DW is a matter of planning, training but also luck with the conditions. To catch the tidal Thames at Teddington just as it starts to go out can mean leaving Devizes in the dead of night. A tail wind and a good flow of water after rain will also help if you have the necessary strength and endurance. The most heart breaking tale of the DW is of Steve Baker and Duncan Capps, who set an unofficial record in 2000, arriving at Westminster 16 minutes before the best time set in 1979. Conditions were excellent but only three hours after starting they started the race it was cancelled due to an accident near Windsor. Baker and Capps were allowed to continue on the understanding they could not set an official record. So if you really want to write yourself into Wiltshire's history books you need to beat 15 hours, 17 minutes and 45 seconds. Or just be amazed that somebody averaged 9mph in a canoe for that long.

Andrew McInerney and Tom Vallings managed it in 25 hours 12 minutes, but some of their better trained compatriots from the military did not. Andrew, a Royal Marine himself at the time, reckons it is a case of "KBO": keep buggering on.

"Our rule was just keep moving east. We were better runners than canoeists so carried the canoe past sections where you get seven or eight locks in a row. 125 miles of rowing I figured would be five marathons back to back, but it is nothing like as tough as that. It is that line from Thackeray: 'To endure is greater than to dare'. Always a good line to throw at special forces with their 'who dares wins' moto. Tom's dad was an Admiral and laid a picnic on for us and it was a case of how fast we could keep moving without being rude. There are a couple of places that you have to be aware could be dangerous, especially in the dark: weirs, a long circular tunnel where no one could see you if you capsized. The support crews are so important: if you miss a meeting point where you were hoping for a Mars bar or espresso, you do feel abandoned.

"Tom was already a great rower and I had every confidence in him. We argued for 125 miles about the physics of going round the bends: whether the short route over shallow water, or the longer way round over deeper water, was faster; but we only had two incidents when we got cross with each other.

"The first was when I feel asleep and capsized us. I was hallucinating about dogs swimming alongside and when I saw Daniel Day-Lewis in his Last of the Mohicans kit on the bank I knew it was going to happen. We rolled over, it was too deep to stand so we had to rock the canoes to get water out of it, or it might break. We got to the bank of a lovely lawn running down from a big house, the security lights came on then we could hear barking and what we imagined were a couple of Dobermans running down to get us. The organisers shouted out for our race number so, at the next stop, Debs (Andrew's wife) had dry clothes and got me running up and down to get some heat back into me.

"Then Tom talked about giving up, and by then your thumbs are red raw, you've got what amounts to nappy rash, everything hurts. At times like that I'll use [Olympic gold medallists and rowers Steve] Redgrave and [Matthew] Pinsentis calls to each other; 'If not now, when? If not us, who?'. All the preparation, the support crew's efforts. So we pushed on and suddenly you come under Westminster Bridge and there's the Houses of Parliament and a bloke in a dry suit on a rope calling 'over here'. I just collapsed into his arms. It is doable, but if I did it again it would be in the class that let you camp overnight and enjoy it a bit more. It did take a while for all the little injuries to sort themselves out after doing it in one hit".

So the 125 mile Devizes to Westminster race is “doable”, but I will add a caveat: Lord Paddy Ashdown completed the DW when he was a Royal Marine, remembering it as “…crippling. We took 25 hours to finish the course, and I can only think of one person in history who has spent a worst Easter”.

Apart from the DW, the Kennet and Avon canal in Devizes is most famous for the short, sharp climb up 16 locks that are part of a total of 29. Despite its magnificent engineering the canal was never really a commercial success, perhaps because it came so late. Completed in 1810, railways were already killing canals as a serious means of transport, and the Kennet and Avon soon had to compete with Isambard Kingdom Brunel’s GWR. The first 22 mile section of the Great Western Railway was ready for service on June 4, 1838 and the line continued to open in stages over the three years that followed. It was so much faster than anything that preceded it that it gave the English language a new word. Today we are more familiar with the use of the word commute to mean travelling to work or, occasionally, to commute a prison sentence by making it shorter. But it was the later usage that was the original, and we get the modern commuter because train travellers’ journey times were dramatically commuted. Watches set by sundials were ten minutes slow by the time commuters arrived in Bristol. Legislation was passed requiring all clocks to be set to the time at Greenwich, something Bristol protested at by giving the clock over their old Corn Exchange two minute hands: the black hand shows the required Greenwich time and the red minute hand shows Bristol time.

The run up to Easter that is Lent also gives us another word, but one that will not affect Wiltshire until the autumn. Carnival is a corruption of Italian for “the meat goes”, and in northern Italy it was a celebration just before the rigours of 40 days and 40 nights of going without meat.

There are good reasons for this, related to our Shrove Tuesday. By now last of the autumn's preserves, especially meat products, need using up. The days are warmer and, without refrigeration, old stores of food might be going off. Ham pancake, anyone?

Wiltshire might once have been famous for her sheep, but gradually the pigs took over. Ham must be the easiest and most successful way easy to preserve meat, and Wiltshire still has houses with a brining bath, carved in greensand stone, sitting unused in cellars. Pig welfare was much worse historically: many houses would have kept a single porker, fed on household scraps. Dispatched in autumn, the winter frosts left to sterilise the sty for a new piglet in March. The pig would have been butchered into parts that needed eating sooner rather than later with the hams – the hind legs – salted and soaked in brine to preserve them for as long as possible. This small scale production stayed with many families until the 1930s but others were more ambitious. Calne in central Wiltshire is remembered for its prodigious pork butchering, although originally it was another market town that had grown from an Anglo Saxon settlement. Calne is set at the head of the River Marden, which flows north to join the Avon on its way the Bristol, there were watermills for cloth factories and, by the eighteenth century, Calne was growing wealthy as a happy consequence of being on the main London to Bristol road.

In the nineteenth century a couple of the town's butchers decided to join forces and by 1889 were selling bacon, sausages and lard wholesale under the brand C&T Harris. Legend has it that most of the pigs were brought over from Ireland, huge numbers passing through Calne on their journey between the port of Bristol and London. Harris's were soon butchering up to 3000 pigs a week and, at its peak, the factory employed some 2000 people locally, turning 5000 pigs into 100 tonnes of pies, sausages and cooked meats every week. Harris developed the Wiltshire cure that used less salt, which was expensive, but still allowed hams and bacon to reach London on Brunel's new railway without refrigeration.

Harris's became Calne, providing everything the town needed including, at one point, a power station. Even in the early 1970s, advertising with the slogan "Wiltshire pigs are happy pigs", Harris's had a national reach. But by then they were just one part of a huge conglomerate, and the end came quickly, with a combination of Britain's economic demise and cheaper Danish bacon. In 1982 the factory closed and was demolished in 1984.

Pigs remain in the Wiltshire landscape, enjoying rooting up their fields and offering a high quality alternative to cheaper imported pork. I think it is the only meat I could never give up, not just for the slow roasts, chops and bacon, but also the range of by-products. It is said that only the squeak is wasted and our local butchers offer brawn (the "head cheese"), sausages (of course) and handmade faggots from the liver for under a quid. Even the blood is used for the under rated treat that is black pudding, the perfect addition to plump scallops.

Sadly Calne's story became an example of what can happen if you put all your eggs (or bacon) in one basket. Calne had nothing else for people and a lack of public transport and the distances to where alternative work might be found brought problems more associated with failing northern cities. One of the biggest studies ever undertaken into depression was based in Calne. It took massive investment, including diverting the river Marden into the town centre, to start to get things back to normal. This for a town that originally had as much going for it than haughty Marlborough further along the road to London.

In the countryside between Wiltshire's market towns the birds start to reappear during March. Blackbirds, with their big eyes the first caller of the dawn chorus, leave the shelter of hedgerows to join the fearless robin out in the open. Although the endless lines of starlings on power lines and their sudden scream into murmarating black clouds that were commonplace thirty years ago have gone, there are successes. When pheasants were brought here for shooting parties, their rapid rate of climb apparently offering marksmen a particular challenge, many of Wiltshire's large birds were hunted to extinction. The clusters of beech trees often seen on Wiltshire's downs were planted by huntsmen, who discovered that beech trees, with their shallow, octopus like roots, could be persuaded to grow up there. Called tumps, these small woods offered shelter for wildlife but, as the Royal Marines taught us in January, hiding in the limited cover of Wiltshire's downs means it is pretty obvious where you are.

Thankfully many species of Wiltshire's larger birdlife has been successfully reintroduced. Watching buzzards' aerobatics to impress a potential mate is fantastic: a bird that can loop the loop! And the red kites you can watch from above from Oliver's Castle are magical, even if finding the gory remains of a blackbird is the price you might pay for reintroducing birds of prey. And then there is the Great Bustard, a mad turkey-like creature that is the world's heaviest flying bird is occasionally glimpsed, although coming round a country lane's narrow turn on a motorcycle to find one running towards you is a wake up call. Watching it run into woodland, listening to the birdsong that has been largely absent from the Wiltshire countryside for six months, you realise that spring is finally here. Things can only get better.

- APRIL -

BUILDING BRIDGES

In April the grand country houses throw their dust sheets aside and put on their cream teas. Peter Mandelson, who was once "intensely relaxed about people getting filthy rich", now frets that some people are just too wealthy. This revelation came after he became a member of the House of Lords and part of a history that tells of a time when the gap between the many and the few was far greater than most of us can imagine.

That these fabulous country houses have to open up to fee paying visitors to pay their own bills is hugely ironic. They were lived in by people who by accident of birth were spared the misery and overcrowding that Thomas Hardy found so fascinating. In a 19th century census a two bedroom terraced house in Swindon had a family of seven – plus a lodger. A seamstress rented a part of the husband and wife's bedroom as "quarters", literally living behind curtains in a quarter of the bedroom. The arrangement was commonplace, especially if a son found a wife but nowhere to live. An arrangement as odd to us today as rattling around forty or so bedrooms just to keep up with the Lord and Lady Joneses.

The design of our grand houses gradually developed a very particular style, largely because nobody wanted something that looked a bit continental Catholic. The trick was to look grand enough to impress, but not so good as to make people in power wonder if you might actually be a Catholic. An ennobled sense of entitlement was also being reined in by the French Revolution, and what that had done for the aristocracy.

But where the English country house was truly unique was in its landscaping. France's troubles kicked off with Marie Antoinette's advice on cake from the grand palace of Versailles. The gardens were supposed to be the greatest in Europe – the French still think they are – but to this English visitor they look like a garden centre that over ordered some square plant pots. English gardens once followed this geometry, especially from the gardens of the Netherlands, but one day we just decided to follow a completely different path. What the English invented became known as the picturesque movement, and is arguably our greatest gift to the world of art and beauty.

William Kent was a painter, greatly influenced by the landscapes he had seen around the ruins of the ancient Greeks and Romans on his Grand Tour. He decided that "all gardening is landscape painting", in an age when "gardening" was reinventing the acres around a country house rather than pulling some weeds. Critic and observer Horace Walpole realised that Kent had "leaped the fence, and saw that all nature was a garden". The English garden was born.

Kent's genius was making a completely invented landscape look as though that was how it had always been. They were designed to be walked around and, while specimen plants could be noted and discussed, the layout was such that it seemed everything had just self seeded. Perfectly. "Ruins" were built in a perfect state of decay, and cottages were built that looked as if they belonged to a woodsman. There are even records of "hermits" being paid to gnaw at a bone by the window, to the amusement of guests as they walked past.

Huge lakes would be dug and filled, appearing to be rivers. This gave the opportunity to build a bridge across them, allowing a change in perspective and elevation, as well as an alternative walking route. Kent's most famous garden at Stowe features a Palladian bridge, one of only three in the country. The other two are in Wiltshire. Well, almost.

Palladian is another very English style, unashamedly stolen by Inigo Jones from Andrea di Pietro della Gondola. Gondola was a sixteenth century architect working under the pseudonym Palladio in northernmost Italy. His work is a stunning argument for simplicity, allowing scale and proportion to speak rather than all the twiddly bits we, and especially the French, were still using 200 years later. When Inigo Jones discovered Palladio on his own Grand Tour he became so obsessed with him that he even changed his signature to mimic Palladio's. Returning to England Jones single handedly changed the way English buildings looked, creating what we call Palladian architecture, because Jones was more than happy to admit his inspiration. The toasted tea cake terraces of Bath are perhaps the finest example, although there are plenty of country houses that prove the point just as well. Where the baroque style (named after misshappen pearls by an unimpressed Victorian) that had gone before was flouncy, florid and boasted of wealth – and possibly worshiping as a Catholic – the Palladian style was sensible shoes. But perfectly made, beautifully finished, bespoke sensible shoes. It was also obviously Protestant and a quiet backdrop for William Kent's idea of a picturesque garden. While the continent remained in love with showing off, England realised that understated beauty with an eye for clever detail was the future.

A fine example of this is the first Palladian bridge Kent built at Stowe to the north east of Wiltshire. Built over a more rustic bridge, the Palladian bit above is part Roman temple, part tribute to the freemasons' art. The oolitic stone from the Bath region (and north west Wiltshire) is so finely layered, limestone created from billions of tiny creatures that lived millions of years ago, that it can be carved in any direction. Although it is a sedimentary rock made up of many layers these are so fine that it does not simply split, like slate. This versatility means it is classed as a "free" stone: a mason was free to choose which direction he carved in. Those who could carve free stone were the finest masons, known as freemasons.

Their secrecy was born of only wanting a few men to learn their skills, allowing them the charge the highest prices of any trade.

Palladian bridges would, therefore, have been expensive, even if the style was deceptively simple. But they allowed a bit of quiet boasting, as well as shelter from rain and private corners where trysts could be tried out. As well as the bridge at Stowe the only others are at Prior Park, just outside the western boundary of Wiltshire close to Bath; and the one in the grounds of Wilton house. The Wilton where the carpets came from, and that gave Wiltshire its name.

Ironically Stourhead gardens, in the southwest of Wiltshire, does not have a Palladian bridge. Oddly because the main house was one of the first country houses built in the new style around 1750, and had some astonishing features in what is probably my favourite landscape garden. This is helped by the fact that dogs are allowed in towards the end of the day and that it has a stunning Temple to Apollo, god of the lunar landings. It was not even designed by a professional gardener, but rather the owner of the house, Henry Hoare II. Henry liked to be known as "Henry the Magnificent" in an era of egos and nicknames. Which brings us to the most famous gardener of them all.

Capability Brown was born Lancelot, and proved to be as brilliant a salesman as he was a garden designer. He had worked under William Kent, but went on to be the most prolific creator of picturesque landscape gardens. His nickname arose from the way he would guide a prospective client around his grounds, talking enthusiastically of the site's "capabilities". The ability to persuade the landed gentry to rip up their formal gardens, lay them mainly to grass, and plant trees that they would never live to see mature was a remarkable feat. Brown could also tell of how the grass would be kept short by sheep, adding yet more wealth to his clients' bulging pockets. To keep those sheep from reaching the house, he would build a retaining wall that held the lawn in front of the house several feet above the grazing below. Thus the landscape seemed to run right up to the house, the drop in the grass barely noticeable until you almost fell into it. At this point most people went “Ha-ha!” which is how the feature got its name.

Capability Brown gardens in Wiltshire include the lower parts and lake of Longleat’s Center Parcs – the beach and zip wire were not his idea – and the landscape of Bowood House in central Wiltshire. Bowood House is gone, although my stepmother has a tiny piece of it. It is a ceiling boss, a gift to her for working as the auctioneers’ assistant when the house was sold off piece by piece. The post war introduction of inheritance tax led to many such peculiarities as families that had been used to wealth for centuries found a new world order. Bowood was sold off piece by piece, and then opened to the public. More common was the mysterious house fire, such as the one which razed Roundway House near Devizes. Stranger was the grand old vicarage near Lyneham I visited in the 1990s. Knowing a little of its history and that it was built in an age when the second son of a wealthy family, denied inheritance of a title and estate but not an income, would take the cloth.

As I rolled along the gravel drive between specimen trees, a visual delight seemed certain. What I got was a very modest Victorian wing, looking a little lost. The main Georgian section had disappeared. It was in the cellar. Really. Opening the door under the stairs should have revealed a staircase: instead the way was blocked by rubble. There was more in the far reaches of the garden. Strange but true.

The reason was nearby RAF Lyneham. After the war people had no wish to return meekly to “service”, having too often experienced officers whose rank reflected a title rather than a talent. And besides, the work gave little time off, even to sleep. In the winter servants were expected to crawl across bedroom floors, lighting fires to ensure their employers didn’t have to wake in a cold room.

Over at RAF Lyneham there was plenty of work with terms and conditions that servants to the local vicar could only dream of. By the 1950s the church gave up trying to recruit and simply demolished the main part of the vicarage and moved a much belittled vicar into what had been the servants' wing. For most of the previously entitled wealthy the post war changes were similarly seismic.

At the other end of Wiltshire one fine country estate had a radical take on coming to terms with the new order. Longleat's resident, Lord Bath, had opened to the public in 1949 as a traditional tourist destination to allow visitors to see how the other half lives (more like the other 0.1% really) but had greater ambitions for his Capability Brown landscape. In 1966 the first British safari park opened, headlined by the lions of Longleat. We were astounded. You only saw lions on television – black and white television, at that - proud beasts under clear blue skies. Or in a zoo, pacing, frustrated at their cruel incarceration, innocent prisoners whose only release could be the death penalty. Suddenly here there were, roaming the magnificent plains of... Wiltshire. Was that David Attenborough you could hear in the background? And lord knows what the lions made of snow, something they had only ever seen from afar, on the fondant capped mountains of Kenya.

Lord Bath created one of Wiltshire's must see destinations, even today when many are able to travel to see lions in the wild. In 1966 it was unimaginable. There is no record of even Lancelot Brown seeing such capabilities in Longleat's landscape when he first visited Lord Bath's ancestor, although Longleat's archives include a letter from the owner begging not to be sent any more tigers as gifts. Yet despite fame as a safari park, Longleat see its future success being more closely associated with its heritage – of which exotic animals are a part – rather than as a theme park. The house is one of England's finest pieces of Elizabethan architecture, and the Capability Brown grounds are of more interest to overseas tourists that the lions. And while Longleat House might be almost 500 years old, the impressive hills that surround it were home to many of our ancestors thousands of years before that, making there plenty to see nearby and tempt visitors into extending their stay in one of Longleat's hotels.

The other truth is that the drive through the safari park can be a mixed bag. The big cats might be in hiding. The monkeys will ruin your car. And you can only go at the pace of the car in front. Years ago, before air conditioning became the norm, I was stuck behind a straggler, with an impatient minibus right behind me. On this rare scorching summer's day the car's temperature gauge moved further and further into the red. The only way to cool the engine was to turn the heating on full blast, since even opening a window a tiny amount had a warden bellowing to shut it from the other side of the fence. Frankly, after an hour, being eaten alive would have been a welcome escape. And the big cats would have had their first taste of cooked meat.

Longleat, like all heritage tourist attractions, has to operate in a market where there are just so many historic places vying for a tourists' attention. Only Italy really has the same density of cultural monuments and, as in Italy, the British people expect them all to be looked after – ideally without troubling the taxpayer. The problem, as in Italy, is that we once had such an extensive and wealthy empire that nobody really expected to come to an end. Once the United States decided they wanted to rule the world, and we decided that we really ought to give people their countries back, the money stopped flowing in from overseas. Luckily an age of cheap airline seats not only meant that we could escape to the sunshine of southern Europe for the price of a gloomy mini-break in Blackpool, it meant the world could come and have a look at the country that invented the way we live now.

The truly amazing thing about Wiltshire is that you can chart that progress, one tourist hotspot at a time. Above the Bratton white horse, where people first built houses and started to farm. The same spot where King Alfred defeated the Vikings and created England. The Magna Carta in Salisbury cathedral that started to dilute a king's power. Civil war battle sites that took that power and gave it to an elected parliament. The grand country houses and their estates that grew rich as we sought the run the biggest empire the world will probably ever see in our own image. This isn't just Wiltshire, it is the way most of the world now runs.

But it was a bumpy ride and, as today, not everybody benefitted. People put their own interests first. When we arrived in India the masters of the empire realised they could buy wheat more cheaply than in Wiltshire and the rest of England's countryside, keeping farm labourers' wages low. The Indian farmers were happy to take the higher prices from the British and let their countrymen starve. It is a credit to the metaphorical builders of bridges who came later that most can put the cruelty of history behind them as a lesson for the future rather than try and erase it. And, indeed, that it is taught in that way: there are still many, many countries that teach lies created as propaganda many years ago in order to keep a population loyal to their leaders and to view outsiders with suspicion. Our own civil war, which in Wiltshire included the biggest cavalry battle of the conflict, was a case of setting those who believed in democratic rule via parliament against those who believed in the rule of a monarch. It is incredible that we managed, eventually, to allow the two to work side by side.

In Wiltshire, as elsewhere, there are many pubs called the Royal Oak alongside the claim that the man who would become King Charles II hid in old oak tree nearby after his defeat in the civil war. It is certainly feasible, if only as an anecdote based upon a tale that started a hundred miles north of Wiltshire. After escaping a battle with his life, the future king was hiding in White Ladies Priory in Shropshire, north west of Birmingham. Along with a few allies he planned to run down to the River Severn, then into Wales and on to France. But the Parliamentarians guessed as much and were guarding his proposed escape route. So instead the royalist escape party fled through Wiltshire, down to Shoreham on the south coast and on to the Isle of Wight and France.

The king's story, told to Samuel Pepys many years later, "was to get up into a great oak in a pretty plain place where we could see round about us, for they would certainly search all the wood for people that had made their escape. [Getting] up into a great oak that had been lopped some three or four years before and so was grown out very bushy and thick, not to be seen through. And there we sat all the day."

And eventually there were, so to speak, bridges built that allowed Charles II to take his place on the throne, while Parliament also retained powers. Charles II was also the catalyst for allowing Catholics to come out of hiding, and the religious tolerance most people accept as fair and proper today. There are those who call our parallel acceptance of monarchy and Parliament, of Anglican and Catholic Christianity as classic English fudges. But surely they are bridge building exercises that allow people to live one way, while accepting we are all different. And that we actually often rely upon one another.

Part of the reason this happened was the Black Death, a plague that some estimate reduced the population of England to just two million souls in the fourteenth century. This swept across the country in waves throughout the 14th Century killing between a third, and perhaps as much as two thirds, of the population. There are stories of villages being burnt to the ground and rebuilt on higher ground, and suddenly no-one wanted to live near the village church with its rapidly filling graveyard. Paranoia and royal proclamation meant that villages became strung out from the church with as much space as possible created between houses. Fireplaces and chimneys were increasingly mandatory, possibly to encourage the clothes of the dead to the burnt.

But in a way many of us should be grateful for the Black Death. Once it had passed even the lowest of the low found they were in demand, and some of the once-wealthy had to start renting their land out. This meant that peasants could rise to tenants and some eventually found that they had occupied land for so long that they effectively owned it. Suddenly there weren't just nobles and peasants but people in between, and the march of the middle class had started.

The Black Death had come from the Far East, via the oriental rat flea, and never really died out in England. The plague returned in waves, holding particularly to overcrowded London. Eventually it led to a complete ban on building in the capital, with James I even requiring some property to be demolished. The plague was only effectively "cured" in London by the Great Fire of 1666, but the rebuilding act that followed didn't just address fire prevention but also the spacing and relationship between houses to try and minimise the spread of disease. From the Black Death on, stone had become increasingly popular, in part because it was considered more hygienic than timber, as was a detached house with a good fireplace. By the eighteenth century even a peasant could aspire to owning a stone house with a good sized garden on the edge of a village, and all due to plague. Even today the plague pits of Wiltshire sit abandoned on the edge of villages, a reminder that we are not as omnipotent as we think.

During Queen Victoria's reign the population of her seat of empire rose from 25 million to nearly 42 million, although the notoriously laissez-faire Victorian business community believed overcrowding in British towns and cities was the "natural order and a handsome state of material progress". Once again, with so many people seeking work, poverty inevitably returned. How quickly we forget.

Compared to the millions killed by disease war is a minor player. Although World war II led to between 50-70 million deaths, that horrendous toll represented less than three per cent of the planet's population. In the fourteenth century alone historians believe perhaps 100 million succumbed to fatal disease, representing possibly a quarter of the people alive at the time. The English civil war was arguably the bloodiest in history and despite the main protagonists being a Norfolk farmer – Oliver Cromwell – and a monarchy based in London, the main fields of battle were in Wiltshire, Gloucester and Somerset. The conflict left some 34,000 Parliamentarians and 50,000 Royalists dead from fighting alone with more than that total killed by disease. At least his would be the last war fought on British soil, but there was very nearly one other that was expected to involve Wiltshire.

The Nazis were expected to make a successful invasion of the south coast of England as early as 1940. Although Dunkirk had been a miracle of logistics that saved much more of the British Army than even Churchill had dared hope, all their equipment had been abandoned in France. The General Headquarters blue line was a defence project that it was hoped would delay the Nazis long enough for us to rearm and launch a counter attack. So the benign waterways between the Bristol Channel and the Thames estuary would become our last stand since the Norman invasion almost a thousand years earlier.

While some of the river stretches could be defended by the navy, the real weak point was the Kennet and Avon canal. Narrow, shallow and well served by bridges it would pose little or no obstacle to a tank advance. That had to change.

It is the pillboxes that I'm most familiar with. Placed along and close to the canal these octagonal brick hideouts were semi buried and by the 1970s only children could squeeze into the overgrown, narrow entrances. Once inside the small horizontal slits intended for machine guns made excellent look outs or the chance the throw stones at confused ramblers. On rainy days they, along with the old shepherd's huts, were our den of choice. They sit unloved today, but unlike some churches that were fired upon in the civil war, thankfully bear no scars from enemy action.

The canal's bridges had "hedgehogs" installed, huge buried concrete mound with holes in that could quickly have vertical metal posts inserted. Access to wider towpaths bridges and were also made much narrower with concrete drums: anything to slow the march into our industrial heartlands. Fortunately they were never needed, but are a reminder that the canal's builders never imagined the British might one day worry about being invaded.

At the western end of the canal, just before Wiltshire becomes Somerset on the road to Bath, there are two aqueducts that carry the Kennet and Avon on its way to the Severn. These wonderful bridges are typical feats of Victorian engineering, from an era when the answer was always yes, even before the question had been asked. After the efforts of the Caen hill locks, how hard could it be to build a couple of bridges to carry the canal to the River Avon and on to the Bristol Channel?

The first aqueduct is at Avoncliff, crossing both the Great Western Railway line and The River Avon, built, along with the rest of the Kennet and Avon canal by John Rennie and chief engineer John Thomas in 1801. It features an incredible arch, spanning 60 feet to leap the Avon in a single bound. The railway line did not appear until 1857, and Brunel considered the tunnels under the aqueducts once of his greatest challenges.

Rennie was born wealthy but would skip school to watch and work with the inventor of the threshing machine, Andrew Meikle.

But Rennie still got into Edinburgh University before moving to the Birmingham area with Boulton and Watt, a steam engine manufacturer. Moving to London and setting up on his own account, the Kennet and Avon canal was his second major project after the Lancaster Canal.

After Avoncliff is Dundas Aqueduct, taking the canal back across the GWR – which was not even planned when the aqueducts were built - and the River Avon. Both aqueducts are stunning, single span, creations and offer excellent sightseeing, walks and cycling. Even narrowboat trips can be had. Rennie, like most Victorian engineers, hated using the Bath stone that is so beautiful in setting sunlight. Whether the stone was used for aesthetic reasons to showcase the Doric, Palladian style architecture or for cost is not certain. Rennie's concerns can be seen in the sagging of the central arch at Avoncliff, which happened soon after construction and thankfully got no worse.

Where the Georgians had loved Bath stone, Victorian engineers loved to use brick, the stronger the better. The way bricks are laid in a regular pattern is called the bond: most modern cavity walls are in simple stretcher bond, with the side ("stretcher") visible and the ends ("headers") hidden. Older, solid wall houses use variations, often using two or three rows of stretcher bond succeeded by a row of header bond. It is the header bond that gives the wall its strength, but also uses more bricks than any other arrangement. For this reason header bond – with no stretchers on show at all – was beloved of Victorian engineers, even when not necessary. Header bond says "I can afford to do this properly, and that is what I shall do." Victorian engineers built things to last.

And they did this all without power tools. The canals were dug by men armed only with picks, shovels and wheelbarrows. These were the navvies – navigators – that would go on to build the railways. To travel on water had long been called navigating, so it seemed natural to call those who created the new waterways navigators, soon abbreviated to navvies, a word we still use today. It was hard, backbreaking, work based on long days and temporary accommodation often in the middle of nowhere. A good navvy was expected to move 20 tons of earth a day, but was also fed well and paid even better by engineers and investors who knew their value. By the time of the great railway expansion in the mid nineteenth century a new railway line needed a speedy conclusion to squeeze out competitors and squeeze on paying commuters. Navvies delivered that and at one time about 250,000 were working in England, around a third of them Irishmen escaping the potato famine at home. As the continent caught up with the British railway boom, many of our navvies moved abroad able to command double what local workers were paid, such was their speed and ability.

The building of the canals taught us everything we needed to cuckold them with the railways. Canals need to be level, and level railways allow faster, more economical trains. Railways need bridges and viaducts, together with the navvies to clear the route. Railways took the industrial revolution and connected it to Britain's towns and cities, especially the ports. And most especially the ports of Bristol and London, a job so important that it was entrusted to England's greatest engineer. And the great engineer thought it so important that he based it in Wiltshire.

Legend has it that Isambard Kingdom Brunel chose Swindon, in north Wiltshire, as the base for his workshops while driving along eating his lunch when he threw half a ham sandwich out of the carriage and declared: 'wherever this sandwich lands we'll build our locomotive repair facility.' And it landed at Swindon. It is a nice story, but in truth the directors of GWR had authorised the building of the new works three months before the Swindon section of the railway opened in May 1841. It was not really at Swindon either: Swindon means swine hill, and given the nickname for the GWR was 'Brunel's Billiard Table' it was never going up a hill. So strictly speaking Brunel's workshops were not at Swindon, initially at least. Brunel needed plenty of land that was going to be easy to buy: his workshops would cover over 300 acres, 73 of them under cover. With over 40,000 workers it soon dominated the local economy and absorbed swine hill to become the Swindon we know today.

Swindon's wealth was from its stone quarry, much used to pave London's streets after the great fire of 1666, so great farming estates were less dominant than further south. Following the old London to Bristol road would have meant negotiating with the wealthy market towns that relied on agriculture and crossing the Marlborough Downs. The owner of Savernake Forest, the marquess of Ailesbury, objected to any railway crossing his land, as he had the Kennet and Avon canal, also once pencilled in for running further north. And by going north, Brunel was also creating the possibility of branch lines to Oxford and Cheltenham. The later would also give access to Wales. For a relatively inexperienced 27 year old Brunel was already thinking big.

North Wiltshire also offers more clay and opportunities to build brickworks. Traditionally bricks would be made close to where they were needed, so heavy were they to transport. The clay used for bricks is found in shallow deposits, known as lenses. Packed into brick shaped wooden boxes, the raw bricks were carefully piled up and covered before being burnt and hardened. Those that broke in the process where know as brickbats and thrown from the pile.

The next stop for the Billiard Table Railway was Chippenham to the south west and so rejoining the London to Bristol road. Here a nine arch viaduct was built from brick to create a railway in the sky. Built in a mix of local stone and English bond brickwork, which runs alternating row of headers and stretchers, it was by far the biggest local structure. Below were muddy tracks used for droving and taking livestock to market. The contrast between a way of life little changed for millennia and the new steam age above could not have been greater. The huge viaduct not only brought Brunel's trains to Chippenham, but also his new brickworks. Chippenham was literally the end of the line for now as Brunel contemplated his greatest challenge: the world's longest tunnel that would be needed to get to Bath. But he knew he would need many more bricks, and that he would have to carry on building bridges.

- MAY -

FOX ON THE RUN

In early May my wife stumbled across fox cubs playing in the garden. It was a rare performance, foxes usually wise enough to keep out of sight but, as the days lengthen, the cover of darkness is too short for our native predators to feast. Foxes will wander by, at a distance, with a surly eye on any humans. Their expression says, "so what? I'm not doing anything wrong", when both sides know out of sight does not mean out of mind. We have lost chickens to foxes when forgetting to lock them in at this time of year, but there are cubs to feed and it was our mistake. Badgers are another thing, never seen but returning each night to try and break into the coop until we replaced it.

With the longer, occasionally sunny, evenings suddenly there is a chance to happen upon other nocturnal predators, including owls. Out foraging for their brood, barn owls know that they will not be able to fly if it rains: their feathers have evolved to allow an eerily silent and deadly flight, at the expense of becoming sodden and worthless if wet. So on a glorious spring evening they will risk being seen by their only predator – man – to be sure of feeding their family. Owls, like most of the larger birds, seem to instinctively realise that humans can use guns to kill them at a distance.

City dwellers seem to imagine country folk as gun totting mavericks trying to deny any wildlife a chance to share their space. But the problem really came with the pheasant shoot beloved of the aristocracy and latter day aspirants. Although introduced from Asia, many specifically for shooting, there are over two million breeding pairs of pheasants in Britain making them to all intents and purposes native. Prized for their rapid climb when disturbed, accompanied by a mad thrashing of wings and a piecing alarm call, they were the perfect test of a marksman's quickness of eye and accuracy of shot: the meat, in truth, is not especially toothsome and, like all game, is so lean that cooking is an art in itself.

When gifted pheasant I will simply cut the breast out with the bird in a plastic bag and dispose of the rest, which does not offer sufficient promise to justify the plucking and gutting. Finely chopped and combined with minced pork, breadcrumbs, eggs, thyme and seasoning pheasant makes a tasty meatloaf. Wrapped in streaky bacon and cooked in a Bain Marie for 30 minutes or so, the meagre breasts can be stretched to a meal for four or even six that does not risk becoming tough and dry as game sometimes can.

In truth, these days most pheasant is shot for the entertainment of the wealthy and then simply dumped into a hole in the ground. Our wonderful local butcher sells farmed pheasant, wary of the risk of shotgun pellets remaining in a bird that ended its days on a shoot. I grew up used to such perils, accompanying my father on nocturnal prowls as designated pigeon retriever from high branches. We killed for the pot, local farmers happy at our incidental pest control. Those who have moral concerns over meat eating – which should be all of us – can eat game with a clear conscience that the animal will have lived a natural life and, if the marksman is worthy of that title, will have known nothing of its demise: by the time there is a gunshot, the animal is already dead. With no natural predators deer especially can overpopulate an area, leaving them with nothing to eat in a hard winter. Culling is only allowed under licence and is far kinder than the factory farming methods domesticated species too often experience. Yes, in an ideal world there would be more wilderness in Britain but, given we already import around a third of our food, that would come at a price. There hasn't been a wild wolf in Wiltshire since around 1290, and perhaps earlier. Free range farmed sheep were plentiful when the Normans arrived, only made possible by the deliberate persecution of wolves. You cannot raise free range livestock in the countryside if there is a large apex predator about.

As it was with pheasants. Anything that might prey on them was driven to extinction by estates keen to organise shoots. Returning to William Hudson's book *A Shepherd's Life*, the author talks of a single buzzard being spotted and how "the days rang with shotguns until it was killed". Eventually even the gamebirds became rarer and rarer. In the end the Game Act of 1831 protected game birds with a closed season when it was illegal to hunt them, offering protection when they were breeding.

A pheasant shoot seems an odd thing the first time you witness it, far removed from the foraging with a twelve bore that I grew up with. While we moved with stealth, pheasant shoots employer beaters to persuade hiding birds to take flight. While we wore the latest waterproofs in the dullest colours, pheasant shooters dress for an Edwardian picnic. Still, in an age of virtual experiences, it is almost real life.

So, as must be obvious, I find the idea of killing for fun bizarre in a world where vegan activists protest in Jamie Oliver restaurants rather than where death takes place. Yes, plenty of countrymen (yes, men) shoot but the majority of participants seem to be involved for the social side: by which they mean networking and deal brokering. LinkedIn looting for the already minted. I once knew someone whose rapid rise to wealth allowed him to attend a shoot with a brand new brace of Purdey shotguns – priced on the "if you have to ask" basis, but think brand new supercar – to the amusement of those who had inherited wealth. One of the old school types, then my boss, explained that Purdeys were like Rolls Royces: something it was crass to buy, but acceptable to have passed down through the family. It is not a lesson I really needed teaching given my salary but, as wealth has accumulated to the City and the Lloyd's crisis of the early 1990s destroyed many who had inherited their money, it is noticeable that such a view would not be recognised on many shoots today.

The birds of prey the gamekeepers drove to extinction have been reintroduced, and the buzzard's distinctive mew is regularly heard, a sound remarkably like that of a flying domestic cat. The red kites were also absent from my childhood, although a sparrow hawk once shook my brother and me as it dived into a nearby hedge and disappeared with its prey. And it is the little prey birds such as kestrels that are so noticeable by their absence. Asking master thatcher Chris Giddings what has changed in his work over the last 50 years, he initially struggles to think of anything.

"Scaffolding" he remembers, tapping a metal post, "couldn't get on with it at first, preferred my old pole ladder, but I'm used to it now." What about the weather, I ask – Chris was half way through his career when I was taught the theory of thatching, which said a full rethatch would last 25 to 30 years, with a new ridge and some patching at half distance.

"We used to reckon on that, but these days it's more like 20 to 25 years. They say it's the pollution" Chris says, waving at the chalk and grass of the Marlborough Downs, which seem an unlikely source of pollutants "but the winters, well we don't get them anymore. I used to sit inside and make spars, but now I buy them in – it's rare to get a winter when we can't work outside. Of course the thatch doesn't like that – it needs a couple of weeks to dry out, and the damp winters we get now let the rot in."

Netting to keep birds off is the only other change that Chris can think of during his lifetime, although even that's less important now that all the birds seem to have disappeared. "Before netting you used to have a gun to keep the sparrows off, but you just don't see them anymore. All the hedges and trees have gone, and so have the birds."

Chatting with Chris makes you realise he's a benchmark for the changes in farming as much as thatching. He has used the same variety of wheat from the same field for just about every job he's ever done, where these days farmers fertilize to encourage initial growth but hybridise and spray wheat to stunt once the ears of grain have formed – long stems make a crop more vulnerable to bad weather, and use up energy that is better expended in a generous grain yield. Chris of course wants long straw, and the ears are just a by-product.

So although many carnivorous birds can survive, thrive even, on carrion, frogs and such, without the "little brown jobs" that were prey for many it is hard to see a way back. And the insects that so many small birds need, especially the swallows and sand martins that start to arrive in May, have also disappeared. Where a long road trip between May and September would involve regular stops to clear a windscreen or visor, those days have gone. It might be convenient for travellers, but those insects are pollinators and if they all go food production will need an army of people with small paintbrushes and large helpings of patience. As the nursery rhyme goes:

Big fleas have little fleas,
Upon their backs to bite 'em,
And little fleas have lesser fleas,
and so on, ad infinitum.

And, as the top of the food chain, it is us who will ultimately pay the price.

All this talk of predators and hunting, with only a brief mention of foxes, brings us to the elephant in the room. Not Anne, the mildly agoraphobic elephant at Longleat, but one of the most divisive issues in the country: foxhunting. It is a topic that seemingly hijacks every attempt to bring rural problems to a national audience and is seized upon whenever it appears in a Conservative manifesto. At every election our local MP, Claire Perry, has a banner erected on the Salisbury road. Every year it gets defaced, and is placed ever higher to defeat the graffiti scribbler. In 2017 reaching it would have necessitated standing on the roof of a van, but the satirist was not to be denied. Under Claire Perry's smiling face was added "eats foxes and hunts the poor". Gifting the opposition such an open goal seems madness.

I have seen two hunts end, both shortly after moving to Wiltshire. The first time was in a friend's garden, when the pack feasted on the family cat. I would have been nine or ten, and was shell shocked not just by the attack, but by everyone's "these things happen" mentality.

The second time was on the Downs above Stanton St Bernard, ironically where Claire Perry would eventually live. The hunt, dressed for a ball, thundered through a wheat field towards us and we gazed down across the open grassland guessing what would come next. Sure enough, a fox leapt from the golden corn's shelter and up, up towards the open chalk land. There was nowhere to hide, no burrow in the dense chalk, nothing to do except run and hope that the chasing pack would give up. It did not.

There are those who claim hunting destroys a chicken killing machine, and merely saves older or weak foxes from a lingering death. Yet foxes are easy to exclude – much easier than badgers – and easy to despatch humanely. In the 1970s we would watch the combine harvester approaching the middle of a near harvested field, while an older watcher would stand, shotgun in hand, ready to take out any fox hiding in the crop. Or simply place bait under a light until the fox gets lazy and fails to sense the gunslinger sitting downwind.

Hunts claim to kill up to 30,000 foxes each year, out of an estimated population of 240,000, but research by Bristol University doubted its efficacy. During the foot and mouth crisis, when there was no hunting, the study claimed the fox population remained static. In truth cars probably kill more foxes than anything else, but fans of hunting remain in love with the tradition with an almost religious zeal. They counter evidence with anecdote, and trump everything with talk of tradition. The only equivalent I have come across is the passion for bullfighting in Spain. Across social status, wealth and gender those who love their sport are united.

In theory fox hunting has been illegal since 2004, but it goes on. I have regularly had a road blocked by an angry man on a horse, forbidding passage regardless of my means of transport. Blocking the Queen's Highway is also illegal of course, but there you go. The claim, if challenged, is that they are hunting a drag, a cloth scented to attract the hounds. A cloth that leaps fences, pushes under hedgerows and zig zags between the fields on either side of the road. Just as a drag behind a quadbike could not, but just as a fox could. After a particularly frustrating episode I took it up with a friendly policeman. "Of course we know it goes on," he laughed. "And we know better than to do anything about it."

Around a hunt will be a huge convoy of fans. Suddenly a dozen or more cars are found abandoned in the middle of nowhere. The range is telling: Range Rovers of course, from the latest and most expensive down to 20 year old wrecks held together with baler twine. Tatty, tiny Peugeot hatchbacks. Little Suzuki jeeps. The fan base is rural, but beyond that guessing who is for or against hunting is nuanced: it is certainly not just the wealthy landowners, seemingly happy to sacrifice their own crops for the entertainment of others. And themselves, of course.

I used to be unequivocally opposed to fox hunting but, in my twenties, became a huge a fan of Ernest Hemingway's novels. Many of these, especially his fabulous *Fiesta: the sun also rises* include what can only be described as love letters to bull fighting. I began to understand the passion for hunting, and a respect of tradition, although I remain opposed to it. But that a largely metropolitan government keeps it on the agenda, raising tempers on both sides, might be a small insight into why electorates the world over vote in a way those in power find largely incomprehensible. Perhaps, like my friendly policeman, they should consider looking the other way when positions are entrenched, and try to build a consensus that unites rather than divides elsewhere. Few wars are won by focussing on battles that look winnable, only to discover the people you think you have liberated actually feel you are an occupying force. To many in the countryside, London looks like a selfish, self-serving aristocracy and the fox hunting ban has become a hook to hang a whole range of grievances on. Which is a huge pity, and incredibly divisive. Which is not helpful in divisive times. I cannot pretend to have an answer, but hopefully at least can offer an insight into the beliefs on both sides.

Fox on the Run was a huge hit for The Sweet, although they were not singing about our hunted friends: fox is also slang for an attractive woman. Recorded in 1974, it was the first of the group's self-penned singles. It got to number five in the UK and US charts, and was the best selling single of 1975 in Australia. Now that's what I call money spinning.

One of the four credited with writing the song is Andy Scott, who moved to All Cannings years ago, my home from the age of eight to 18. Although he looked the seventies pop star, white hair hanging down his back, he was quickly assimilated by his new home. Drinking in the local pub I used to collect my grandmother's sherry from - no proof of age required, although I was obviously not even a teenager - Andy managed that outsiders' trick of fitting right in while trying to make life better for his adopted neighbours. When both he and the landlord of King's Arms – as it still is – were diagnosed with prostate cancer they decided, alongside treatment, they would fundraise for cancer related charities: Rock Against Cancer was born in 2010.

The idea of holding a concert in a field behind a rural pub that featured international stars was not as far fetched as some might think – after all, Glastonbury is only 50 miles to the west – and Andy Scott had an impressive address book. But Glastonbury has always been about turning a profit, where rock against cancer expected performers to play for little or nothing. Remarkably then just three men - sound engineer John "Grubby" Callis, Andy Scott and landlord Richard Baulu put on the first show in 2012. The performers introduced by Bob Harris included Brian May, Midge Ure, Mike and the Mechanics, Tom Robinson, the Strawbs and, of course, the Sweet. £25,000 was shared between two cancer charities, and another £5000 donated to the village parish for their support and to fund other events.

The show became an annual event and was initially a victim of its own success. Queues for the beer tent were legendary, eventually drinking it dry. Parking was problematic, as was increasing the village's population several fold for a day. But Andy Scott and his team listened and learned: volunteers manned the car park, and traffic lights were hired to manage the hundreds of cars navigating often unfamiliar narrow lanes. Staff by the beer tents ran the queues with fairness and speed. Wadworth's brewed an ale just for the concert. Even the cynics started to come, partly because every year the weather just got better. In 2016 the event was sold out, featuring Marmalade, 10cc and a brilliant set by Suzi Quatro. £40,000 was raised bringing total donation from Rock against Cancer to over £152,000 in four short years.

But in 2016 it rained, rained and then rained some more. By the time darkness fell half the audience must have left. For me fine company, great music, pizza and beer were reason enough to stay. For others the fear of not being able to drive their car from the field it was parked in was reason enough to leave. Some of the food vendors found they were indeed stuck by the end of the night. Being the countryside a tractor was eventually found to extricate them, but it was a sorry tale they would tell anyone who would listen. Ironically the date of the concert had been shifted from its usual spot by a wedding that would use the field in sunshine the next weekend, although there was not a blade of grass to be seen.

The lead up to the 2017 Concert at the King's was the driest winter and spring I can remember. Hazy May mornings, like childhood summers, drifted into blue skies. The Met Office website continually threatened downpours, but the 80% chance of rain would melt away with the cloud cover. Grass would not grow, and then bolted into tall seed heads: great if you hate mowing the lawn, but threatening ruin for our local shepherd. Roy Kyte adopted New Zealand's practice of early shearing this year, near worthless fleeces taken early to avoid having to shear shortly after the ewes have lambed. Our newly near-frost free winters mean the sheep are hardly inconvenienced by being rid of their winter coats.

Originally sheep only had what we would recognise as a fleece on one side of their body, allowing a flock to huddle together against icy winter winds. About 8,000 years ago our ancestors started domesticating them, originally simply plucking the fleece to make early woollen clothing. Gradually selective breeding gave some sheep better and bigger fleeces that covered most of their body, while the sheep that did not do likewise became dinner.

Sheep were one of the first animals we domesticated, making us farmers in a fixed spot rather than nomadic hunter gatherers. Babylon, the ancient Mesopotamian city that might be regarded as the birthplace of human civilisation, used to be thought to be named after the gate of god. Some now think Babylon meant "land of wool" and, like Wiltshire, created its wealth from fleeces and weaving. That Babylon is now a complex of ruins in the centre of what we call Iraq, guarded as much for the oil pipeline that runs though it as for its history, is a lesson worth remembering.

By the Bronze Age sheep as we would recognise them were widespread throughout western Asia. From here they were traded to northern Africa and to Europe. Europe quickly took up the cause of an easily domesticated creature that could provide not only meat and milk, but also wool. Classical Greek records from circa 500 BC detail selective sheep breeding and wool processing, while Roman writings describe in detail the sheep breeding processes and fabric production, and suggest the existence of flocks of up to 10.000 sheep. By then there were already sheep farms in Wiltshire, and the demonising of the wolf. The ease with which sheep could be herded made them equally easy prey, which is why our island race set about eradicating wolves and forests rather than relying on a boy who may or may not cry wolf. Our local farmers now use alpacas to keep their flock from harm. Alpacas are llama-like watchtowers, peering over gates and hedges for anything that might wander into their territory.

One of my favourite evening walks takes the dog down a cutting to the railway. Stock fenced on both sides and gated to the railway, the dog can potter around, or bark at teasing squirrels, while I watch Roy's flock, and the effects of the setting sun. During May I had been admiring a basking red deer, rare in these parts, burnished copper in the low evening sun. My wife thinks I am just watching a roe deer in its mating colours until she joins me on the walk.

A plaintive war cry goes up, sounding just like a strangled sheep. Relived to find the dog has not found a way out of the cutting, we see an alpaca chasing the red deer at speed, until the deer leaps the fence and melts into the woods. The alpaca trots haughtily back to its look out post, obviously pleased with the encounter. I do not see the red deer again.

Providing predators can be kept at bay, sheep are almost ridiculously easy to farm compared to other livestock. Pigs can bite off a human limb, and cattle are the biggest killer in the countryside: a rambler caught between a cow and her calf is asking for trouble. Pigs and cattle also need shelter, while sheep can often mange without. Sheep are less picky eaters than cattle or horses, and can eat shorter grass so can follow cattle onto a pasture. Cows use their tongues to grab longer grass and then bite it off: sheep just mow away. Being much lighter than other livestock, sheep will cause less damage to a wet pasture. And chickens are almost as bad as pigs, eventually turning pasture into a worthless mud bath.

But livestock needs vegetation, and vegetation needs rain. The 2017 Mayday Bank Holiday had torrential downpours (of course) but this just ran off the parched and compacted land. The dry spell was reinstated as soon as people returned to work and the wilderness of Wiltshire, such as it is, sprung into a growth spurt that suggested it knew reproduction opportunities would be few and far between. Bright green growth showed everywhere, hawthorn erupting into massive clear white blooms. Birds dart in and out of hedgerows, filling the air with song. Even when you know that birdsong lyrics either mean "fancy a fling?" or "get off my land!" does not detract from something that has been missing from the air for nine or ten months.

And that great vision of fecundity that is the rabbit is everywhere. Hovering near to their greensand burrows, even our lurcher cannot catch them despite his new found early crawl approach. But even a 40 mph dash over fifty yards is no match for a leisurely five feet hop into an underground sanctuary.

While the rabbits enjoy the grass between the sunshine buttercups, in the woods the bluebells are the best ever. We walk with a thermos to nearby Oakfrith woods just to sip coffee and contemplate the swathes of indigo. Driving to Lacock, Mediterranean blue waves from below the still bare oaks on Bowden Hill. In Savernake Forest the bluebells are so dense and widespread it is as if you could go barefoot and paddle in them. Purists complain that Spanish bluebells, often grown in gardens, are diluting our native plant, but it is still special. The Spanish interlopers lack our original intensity of colour but are more easily identified by their blue pollen – it is a creamy white in British bluebells. Even so, almost half the world's bluebells are in Britain. They thrive in deciduous woodland, sometimes also along hedgerows, taking advantage of spring sunshine and pollinators before the canopies above them come into leaf.

All parts of a bluebell are poisonous to humans. Despite this the plant's sap was used to bind the spines of books and to set feathers upon arrows, known as fletching. That may be the origin of the surname Fletcher, although others say it is from Fleischer, the German for butcher. Bluebell bulbs were also crushed into starch for the ruffs of Elizabethan collars. Any medicinal use is limited, presumably because the plant is toxic. Dried it was recommended in tiny quantities for vaginal discharge, and Lord Alfred Tennyson believed bluebell juice could save you from a snake bite. But then Tennyson was a man prepared to try many things. Muntjac, the small demon like deer introduced by the Victorians and widespread in Wiltshire, can happily graze on bluebells, adding to their mystique.

By the middle of May our local butchers, who rear their own cattle, have joined the shepherds in worrying about the lack of rain. And then, in the third week of May, at last it rains. Gently at first, allowing the ground to soften and drink in the heavier rain that eventually comes. The cow parsley goes ballistic, in days growing from being a lace umbrella in the lower reaches of the hedgerows, to suddenly towering over me at over two metres high.

And so back to Concert at the Kings 2017. There are noticeably fewer in the crowd after last year's washout, but there is a sort of returners pride among the regulars. John Coghlan's (Status) Quo open, belting out Rick Parfait's *Rain*. The crowd cheer at chorus refrain, *I can live without the rain.*

Perhaps we can, but not today. The rain gets heavier, and the food trailers are glad to be at the top, rather than bottom, of the field this year. It is nothing like as bad as the previous year, and Andy Scott is on top form. Guardians of the Galaxy part two, a high octane superhero film fantasy, used one of his hits for its cinema trailer and as track two on the fast selling soundtrack release. Suddenly it is not just seventies nostalgia that people are dancing to, as teenagers push to the front to see what they think of as a new track for their latest must-see movie. As the sparkling night reflects the fast moving lights, the Pewsey Vale gets to appreciate a revitalised *Fox on the Run.*

- JUNE -

ROMANCING THE STONES

June is when you can wake in the light of early morning, and safely turn over and go back to sleep. June is when you can sit in the garden late into the evening, listening to the last of the birdsong and marvel at the beauty of an English garden. As it finally darkens the swallows and sand martins are replaced by bats feasting on flying insects. Beekeepers might talk of the June gap, when nature takes a break from providing flowers for the pollinators and nectar gatherers, but an English garden is an idealised version of nature so there is still be plenty to enjoy.

Apart from a school exchange visit to France aged 13, I never travelled abroad until I joined P&O's magnificent merchant fleet four years later. My first mentor was a Kenyan third mate who had not visited Britain before. He found our long summer evenings creepy, as if an evil nanny was refusing to turn the bedroom light out and instead taunting with a slow motion dimmer switch. But when we visited Kenya it was my turn to be surprised: the first mate called out to get the ship secured within fifteen minutes rather than rely on floodlights. Given it was still broad daylight it seemed overzealous but, sure enough, fifteen minutes later it was completely dark. Ever since then I have cherished our June evenings and their gradual descent through an evening of scents and sensations until it is finally time for bed.

But for others June in Wiltshire means the summer solstice. These days it is routinely front page news, attractive young women smiling at the stones, in the same way newspapers report exam results and Glastonbury. For many years it was a rather less settled affair, a game of cat and mouse between farmers, the police and the hippy travellers who came, to Stonehenge especially, for the summer solstice.

Back then I was just another teenage motorcyclist, and our relationship with the police was not unlike that of a farmer and a fox. The farmer knows the fox is capable of taking his chickens, but does not know which fox needs to be dealt with. Similarly the traffic police knew that while young motorcyclists might obey all the rules of the road when watched, just because you are not doing anything wrong at the minute does not mean it is not worth following you, or pulling you over for a roadside check. Getting away with it is not the same as innocence.

But around the summer solstice the police had other fish to fry. The area between Avebury and Stonehenge – where I lived and rode – became a sort of giant snakes and ladder board, with the police trying to push the travellers back wherever it was they had come from, before another convoy of dilapidated camper vans and converted small lorries would reappear somewhere else, even closer to a stone circle. Farmers would place their largest pieces of farm machinery and tree trunks across every field entrance, trying to anticipate where the incomers might try and set up camp. None of the travellers' vehicles were taxed, so presumably they were uninsured. Judging by the huge barrels of cider on board it seems possible that drink driving laws were being flaunted, and many vehicles had bald tyres and seemed to be held together by luck and ley lines. But, as with fox hunting, the police were seemingly not interested in illegal activity, just determined to keep travellers from becoming settlers by the stones. On the solstice evening itself riot gear would be donned as the battle reached its climax.

Then, next day, apart from a few revellers sleeping off their hangovers as near to the stones as they had been able to get, the travellers simply evaporated. The police were as mystified and as relived as the rest of us. And so it would continue, every year the weary preparations for battle, the games of cat and mouse, and then a return to normal.

Until, eventually, the police had a flash of brilliance: just let the travellers have their day in the setting sun. Partly driven by the cost of trying to police the solstice, it was a eureka moment. No more chases around the Wiltshire countryside, no more cancelled leave. Also, letting the travellers into the stone circles meant you knew where they were.

An unexpected side effect was that curious locals, especially teenagers, started to join the incomers. Then the portaloos and car park attendants arrived and bingo: the hippy travellers were swamped by a middle class wanting to do something a little edgier than invite friends round to dinner. The solstice at Stonehenge especially now has more of a festival vibe than alternative lifestyle edge, so much so that Stonehenge's money grabbers – sorry, guardians – English Heritage are thinking about charging for admittance to what is currently Stonehenge's only free access day. Almost as soon as the sun rises after the solstice English Heritage are fussing to get people out so that they can restore the stones to their status as a sacred cash cow, and people who are unconscious are laid in a nearby verge with their bottle of cider held to their chest. It is quite a sight.

And yet the wholesale fascination with Stonehenge is comparatively recent. It has been part of an airfield, and nobody batted an eyelid when what is now the A303 was turned into a major through route alongside it. The fuss over this bottleneck on England's main route south west is largely a function of dual carriage-waying this short stretch being resisted at every turn. Even talk of a tunnel was immediately met with outrage, as so much is these days, yet the constant jams and use of nearby village lanes as a rat run does far more environmental damage. Plus a tunnel would mean even more people would have to pay English Heritage to see it. But my favourite objection, courtesy of a caller to Jeremy Vine's Radio 2 show, was that a tunnel would disturb the energy lines that so many healers rely upon. Almost as funny as the Druids' claims over Stonehenge, despite it being built millennia before they got involved.

In the January chapter I argued for respect of the beliefs of our forefathers, but not that they were right. My first day, aged six, at a Catholic school, involved being read Genesis by one of the sisters at the convent. Even then I was excited by the possibilities of science – well, the TV programme Thunderbirds, really – but the idea of just wishing for stuff to happen, and then seeing it was good, did appeal. Everything done in six days, then a day off. Lovely.

Oddly the next lesson was science, and how the solar system was created over billions of years as superheated materials coalesced and settled into stable orbits thanks to the effects of gravity. So I did what any geeky kid did: stayed behind afterwards and quizzed the teacher. Her answer started with "do you know what an allegory is?"

I soon did. It is telling stories to explain something. And that is fine with six year olds. Since then I have swung between believing in something higher and complete atheism. Eventually I settled at agnostic, believing that certainty is impossible and that being convinced there is no god is almost the same thing as being convinced there is. I happily say grace before a meal with a friend who believes the bible is the literal word of God, and am delighted to celebrate Christian events as part of my heritage. Even our children are christened, because that is our tradition. Plus there is Blaise Pascal's point that not believing carries no benefit, especially if you die and find there really is a heaven – and a hell.

One of the first premises of science and philosophy is that you cannot prove a negative, and so science will always be our current best guess. But if science can measure gravitational waves it could measure any energy or lay lines around Stonehenge. During the course of the "long 18th century" (between about 1685 and 1815) European philosophy and science were radically overhauled – invented, really - in a period we call the Enlightenment. For the first time a handful of people realised that things could be studied and organised, that an idea could be floated and then be tested and peer reviewed. That human knowledge could be built up, stone by stone, and people invited to build it higher, alter it, or knock it down altogether. You just had to be prepared to convince the people who had gone before and – this is the hard bit – to have learnt what was already known. No believing required, just an ability to explain logically how things have come to be. Which partly explains why I have read the bible a couple of times.

So take archaeology, a science that started within Avebury's magnificent stone circles, ditches and banks. John Aubrey was born just to the west of Chippenham in 1626 to what we might now call landed gentry. He is credited with discovering Avebury, as if a collection of stones weighing up to a hundred tonnes in a 300 metre wide circle could be missed. Like much of Stonehenge, Avebury was built using the boulders of silicified sandstone that were scattered about parts of Wiltshire. They are the remains of a layer of rock that once covered large parts of southern England and it was not just our ancestors who were fascinated by the random scattering of huge and immensely dense stones across the chalkland. William Stukeley, who built on Aubrey's work at Stonehenge especially, thought that these sarsens had been gradually pushed out of the chalk by the earth's rotation. But then he was a friend of Isaac Newton, famous for his thoughts on gravity: it was Stukeley who wrote the falling apple story, which is probably apocryphal. Stukeley was a fellow of the Royal College of Surgeons as well as the Royal Society, a brilliant thinker but also one of the first people to propagate the myth connecting the druids and Stonehenge. He thought Stonehenge might be some 2000 years old, much older than his contemporaries believed, and so built when the druids were a significant force. But we now know Stonehenge is at least 4500 years old, largely thanks to carbon dating of the antlers that helped create it.

Sarsen is a Wiltshire corruption of Saracen, the enemy in the crusades, but a word that came to simply mean foreign, as in "not from round here" as locals say today. Sarsen masons became as important as the later freemasons, cracking the rocks into blocks. Although modern research has led us to believe the sarsen stones are the remains of Wiltshire as it was millions of years ago, Sir Christopher Wren, architect of St Paul's cathedral, wondered if they had been thrown from a volcano. This is the nature of science: put an idea up, ideally to the Royal Society, and try to find a consensus in an academically rigorous way.

This is where Aubrey, another fellow of the Royal Society, started something new. He started recording stuff, even if he was infamously poor at finishing projects, but at least offering it to other like minded souls for appraisal and comment. He wrote a history of Wiltshire, perhaps the first to do so. He wondered about why Avebury was there, rather than just accepting it was. These seem obvious approaches to us now but were revolutionary at the time. This is why Aubrey is often referred to as the father of archaeology.

It was doubly fortunate that he recorded Avebury's layout because by the eighteenth century the stones were being taken down for building. For centuries the traditional Wiltshire cottage was made of chalk with a thatched roof. But a rapid increase in demand for housing meant that in Avebury the locals started eyeing up the sarsen stones and thinking that they would make much more solid walls than chalk ever could. It also saved the bother of having to quarry the chalk. This however turned out to be a bad idea, even before the days of academics and planning officers who would become apoplectic if you smashed up a Neolithic standing stone to build your house.

Almost as soon as these stone houses were built the occupiers started talking of them sweating. We now know it was just condensation, something never seen on chalk or plaster. Water would seem to pour out of the heart of the stone and run down the inside walls and, in an age when people really believed in witches, ghosts and fairies this must have seemed a very spooky thing.

The "sweating" might even be connected with a spate of tipping over and burying the stones, which made Aubrey's records essential when Alexander Keiller decided to put the fortune generated by his family's marmalade business into restoring Avebury. In 1922 he and another famous archaeologist, O. G. S. Crawford, flew over and photographed potential archaeological sites in south west England, publishing their work as *Wessex from the Air* in 1928. Avebury featured heavily.

Keiller can fairly be described as the man who saved Avebury. He bought the site and the land around it, quickly setting to restoration and examination of the area. He erected posts where stones had been removed, and exhumed stones that had been buried and returned them to their original place. Why the stones had been buried is a mystery: airbrushing of a pagan past by Christians and simply clearing the land for farming are the most likely suggestions.

Keiller's first major excavation at Avebury was in 1937, the first of three that ended with the outbreak of war. In 1938 he discovered human remains under an especially big stone. Initially it was assumed the victim had been crushed to death during the burying of the stone, and his rare and valuable scissors and French and English coins dating to the 14th century led to speculation that he was a travelling barber-surgeon or tailor. But when the skeleton, once thought lost in the war, was rediscovered in the Natural History museum in 1998 it was realised it lacked any crush injuries. The unfortunate man was buried under the stone deliberately and, given that he was buried with his coins and scissors, foul play seems unlikely. Perhaps he died of the plague, and his buriers were fearful they would catch his disease. Yet he would surely have been interred in consecrated ground.

Which leaves an intriguing possibility. The only people denied a Christian burial were those hanged for murder or who had committed suicide – and, of course, non-Christians. Some have suggested a Jewish tailor, but that community did not really come to prominence in England until the eighteenth century. But it is plausible that a "Saracen" was buried under this sarsen stone.

The Second World War ended excavations at Avebury, with Keiller joining the special constabulary at Marlborough. Eventually he would sell his site to the National Trust at a price that simply reflected the price of farmland, taking nothing for its heritage value or Keiller's investment in it.

The landscape around Avebury is almost equally spectacular as the stone circles, ditches and banks. There is no obvious single viewpoint, so it rewards walking around, which costs nothing. Or you can leave via avenues of stones including one predicted by Stukeley to Beckhampton. Then there is West Kennet Long Barrow, built almost 6000 years ago, and used for perhaps a thousand years as the last resting place of at least 46 souls.

But perhaps most vexing of all is Silbury Hill, the largest man made pile of earth in Europe. Over 40 metres high - about the size of an Egyptian pyramid for "was god an astronaut?" conspiracy theorists – and it has resisted erosion despite spending some 4500 years in the Wiltshire countryside. The first attempt at understanding it was in 1776 when the Duke of Northumberland brought in Cornish tin miners to sink a shaft into the very top of the hill.

The Duke's efforts left him none the wiser, and the same has proved true for all subsequent excavations. Really all we know is that it was built in three steps, as a sort of tiered cake of chalk covered with soil and rubble.

During one excavation around 1970, when public access was encouraged, my brother and I sat on the top of Silbury Hill seeing who could throw stones the furthest. The shape of the hill meant we couldn't see where the stones were landing and eventually we heard a yelp and an archaeologist shouting something young boys shouldn't hear. He chased us off and we are still not allowed to return, an embargo placed on walking up the hill to protect it, although the worn paths tell that people still do.

Oh, and Peter Gabriel sung about Solsbury Hill, not Silbury (or Salisbury) as some mishear. Gabriel's hill is near his recording studio between the Wiltshire border and Bath. It's not man made.

Silbury Hill predates the avenues, but not the earliest parts of the Avebury circle. To confuse us further evidence of an inner square at the heart of Avebury's circles has recently been confirmed, that Keiller dismissed in 1939 as the remains of a medieval cart shed. Since a square of standing stones would be unique the wonder now is: could the square be the remnants of a building that was at the very centre of Avebury, and the reason for its existence? As ever, new discoveries just seem to present more questions.

And so to the most famous stone circle in the world, Stonehenge. Almost certainly originally built in one of the few low lying areas of England that were not then covered by forest it has swung from being highly valued to pretty much ignored throughout its history. Julius Caesar and his fellow writers started the myth that it was built by Druids, a Celtic religion prevalent in the area around 55BC when the Roman invasion started. But the Druids, like so many, had a belief system based around the ways of the forest and, anyway,

Stonehenge was 2000 years old by the time Caesar saw it and apparently abandoned.

Our father of archaeology, John Aubrey, repeated the Roman stories when he surveyed Stonehenge. He was the first to try and understand what Stonehenge would have looked like when it was completed, although the consensus now is that it probably never was finished. The places where missing stones or timber posts are recorded are still known as Aubrey holes. Aubrey thought the circle was pretty new when the Romans discovered it and even William Stukeley, who thought Stonehenge was perhaps 450 years old when the Romans wrote of it, also became convinced it was a Druids' den. And the story has stuck. Really all we know is that it allowed its builders – and there were a lot of them – to determine the timing of the summer and winter solstice, and that it was the winter solstice that was when the big celebration was held. So we will return to Stonehenge in December and for now leave it to the revellers currently romancing the stones.

- JULY -

UNCIVIL BEHAVIOUR

How one of the bloodiest wars in history, a war between a London based king and his parliament led by a Norfolk farmer, came to be fought mainly in Gloucestershire, Somerset and Wiltshire seems at first a mystery. Indeed, at the time, it was assumed the battles of the English civil war would remain, as we might say today, London-centric. But, as today, the battles soon became an opportunity for grudges to be aired and old scores settled. Monarchs too often had an overblown sense of entitlement and a lack of insight into how their power was really conferred. Inevitably this led to conflict, and the English civil war was the biggest of them all, with the battle of Roundway Down in the heart of Wiltshire being a central plank of the conflict.

The Norman's had created what we now call the feudal system, establishing rights over land and the obligations between the nobility, the monarch and those who worked and lived on the land. These included obligations to fight, since there were no standing armies, and – of course - to pay taxes. There was also the church, often as powerful as and richer than the monarch. So, in the name of getting things done, meetings between nobles, church leaders and the monarch would be held. It was these great councils that were the seeds of our parliament, although even by the outbreak of war in 1642 parliament was only convened at the king's pleasure – in other words, when he wanted money.

In 1215, the nobility had King John agree that no new taxes could be raised without the agreement of a council. This obligation was the Magna Carta, the finest example of which is displayed at Salisbury Cathedral, and this is where we started to unpick an English monarch's absolute power, previously considered to be a divine right. Who would have thought that over 400 years later it would crystallise into a civil war?

Of course, if a monarch did not need to raise extra taxes, it was possible to rule without parliament. Charles I managed this for eleven years, essentially by making peace with France and Spain, so saving the costs of war. But that did not stop parliamentarians meeting, growing ever more frustrated at what they saw as eleven years of tyranny. Of more concern was that the Protestants suspected Charles of preparing to return England to Catholicism. Yes, religion and war, those old bedfellows. Charles found himself at the mercy of uprisings needing to be quelled, especially in Ireland, and there was an ambitious Scotland to deal with. So Charles was forced into dealing with a by now mutinous parliament with eleven long years spent compiling a wish list that would need to be satisfied before any talk of raising taxes.

Charles finally realised a great rebellion was on the cards and that the parliamentarians had built a powerful and dangerous power base in London. Fleeing to the north of England to try and build a new seat of influence in March 1642, Charles started raising an army. The parliamentarians did the same and the two clashed in the first battle of the English civil war at Edgehill in Warwickshire. Still nowhere near Wiltshire.

But Wiltshire was a gateway to the port of Bristol, and still wealthy on the profits of wool. Cloth for uniforms and munitions' fuses were in the county. Many Royalist foot soldiers were Cornish, so had to cross the county to reach their king. Yet large swathes of west Wiltshire, Somerset and south Gloucestershire were solidly parliamentarian, as were most of the ports and the clothing towns, which were largely populated by Protestant puritans. Drifting away from these strongholds moderate royalism prevailed, especially in the country estates and market towns, making the area the fault line of the different beliefs that ignited into the war.

From our perspective the English Civil War does look more like a succession of grudge matches rather than a war. Battles took place on a pretty ad hoc basis, as one group would chase another down, fight for victory – and then leave for more of the same, rather than trying to secure control of an area. And at the heart of it was one group of wealthy landowners fighting another wealthy landowner to determine who controlled the country. Why this mattered to the foot soldiers is moot, some of who would have been displaced by the enclosures and, regardless of who won, would, in the short term at least, see no change in their lives. Yet in our largely secular age it is hard to relate to a society who believed absolutely in an afterlife and a control by higher, hidden powers. We do not have to look far today to find young men with a fervent belief, and sense of being pushed aside, which propels them to violence and war. Perhaps we were once like that.

Among those who might become foot soldiers there was much to be angry about. The enclosure of common land was well underway, displacing families whose ties to the land went back generations. Protestant Christianity might have been the official religion but it was not just Roman Catholics who were unhappy about this. Many still held pre-Christian beliefs and witch trials and hanging of those found guilty were still well known. While there was a strong belief in witches and their powers – that they could adopt the shape of an animal was widely accepted – there was also misogyny at play. Midwives and healers were often seen as having knowledge that only men should hold, leading to suspicion and mistrust. This was an age when most men had no doubt they were superior to women, and that a clever woman must be using magic to be better than a man – and that such an accusation could hang her. The signs of this part of our history remain plain to see: Hillworth Road in Devizes used to be called Gallows Ditch, and the imprint of the ducking pond is still visible. This was where witches were hanged and buried, alongside the suicides. And from here, next to the Norman castle, the outline of Roundway Down was clearly visible just a mile or so away.

Technically Roundway Down is topped by a univallate hillfort, meaning it has outer ramparts – walls, if you like – around a depression. Roughly triangular with the downs behind, gentle slopes towards Avebury on one side and a steep scarp to the south west, there was little chance of creeping up on the occupants. Like the other hill forts we have seen above scarps, this would have made it easy to defend, implying that attacks on these ancient settlements were expected.

The design of hill forts was an arms race against the development of the slingshot, the attacking marauders weapon of choice, and eventually hill forts would develop inner rings to catch any shots that flew over the outer rampart. Pottery of the Bronze Age, Iron Age and the time of the Roman occupation have been found on Roundway Down, so it survived as someone's home for thousands of years, before people moved down to the fertile plain below.

While Roundway Down might have seen clashes in prehistoric times, they could not have been on the scale of the battle of Roundway Down, the biggest cavalry encounter of the English civil war. It became such a talking point that locally the site became known as Oliver's Castle on the assumption that Oliver Cromwell had personally prepared his troops for battle here. In fact Cromwell came nowhere near, but it has been suggested that some of the prehistoric earthworks are in fact parliamentarians digging in ready for battle.

The 4500 or more men preparing to fight would have outnumbered the population of the market town of Devizes 200 feet below.

The views from here are fabulous, but the parliamentarian forces were more interested in holding the highest ground available and being able to avoid a royalist ambush. Their previous battle had been on a similar landscape and, although historians conclude the parliamentarians had lost that engagement, given the loses inflicted on the royalists Cromwell's men might have seen it as a victory.

That battle had been just five days and twenty miles ago. The royalist commander Ralph Hopton had marched his Cornish infantry into Somerset, combining with forces sent by the king, hoping to create an army that could gain control of the west country. They first sparred with the parliamentarians, led by Horton's old friend William Waller, at Lansdowne, just north of Bath. There were almost 10,000 men on each side. The population of Wiltshire was only 113,500 at the time.

The royalist victory, fought on the clear open slopes of Lansdowne Hill, came at a dreadful cost. By the end of the day (5th July 1643) the royalists had lost as many as a thousand men, where Waller had sacrificed fewer than a hundred. Unsurprisingly, he gave chase as Hopton's men fled to the sanctuary of Devizes castle. Hopton had been injured and almost blinded in an explosion which also left the royalists desperately short of ammunition. Bedding was collected in St John's church, which still has the scars of gunshot on its eastern wall. Devizes was not easily defended, and the royalists were reduced to felling trees as makeshift barricades. A cannonball from the siege was found years later in St James' church tower, and Waller was confident his army, even if now halved in size and settling in for a siege, would have no difficulty finishing off fewer than 2000 royalists hiding in the castle.

But surely Waller should have expected Charles to send additional men to support Hopton? Waller subsequently blamed the outcome of the battle on parliamentarians not doing the same for him. Realising he would need to storm Devizes before the reinforcements arrived, or head off those reinforcements, on Friday, 10th July he dug his troops in at the top of Roundway Down. He wrote to parliament that "the job was all but done" - after all, Waller had a fine record of victories and had not really lost at Lansdowne, dramatically reducing a royalist force that had fled into hiding. He had eight cannon, his enemies had none, and he had 2500 cavalry and almost the same number of foot soldiers. He would handsomely outgun the relief force.

Lord Wilmot had raised 1500 fresh cavalry in Oxford, and Prince Maurice another 300. They rode towards Devizes, the news of which allowed Hopton to release his troops. Although Wilmot and Maurice had a journey of 40 miles ahead of them, Waller's men were already exhausted and hungry.

As well as wanting the high ground, Waller also needed the open spaces that would allow his cavalry room to manoeuvre. With huge irony the hedgerows added during the enclosures in the valleys below would be no friend to the parliament that had granted the rights to enclose. Hedges do not help prosecute battles when you are relying on galloping horses.

On Monday 13th July the royalist reinforcements rode along the Wansdyke, at roughly the spot where I would stop to watch the giant John Deere tractor well over 300 years later, half way between Devizes and Avebury. They realised that battle was to be joined on Roundway Down, headed up what is probably the shallowest approach to the parliamentarian encampment, and immediately charged.

The parliamentarian ranks, shaken by repeated royalist charges, finally broke and fled as Waller called for retreat in the hope they might regroup on a wider battlefield. Those who tried to escape by riding directly away from the royalist charges found themselves confronted by the unrideable scarp, tumbled down, breaking many riders' and horses' necks and giving the name Bloody Ditch to the field below. Others just scattered, especially when they realised Hopton's men were marching up from Devizes. The foot soldiers who stood their ground were slaughtered. Lord Wilmot's royalists had secured what is widely accepted as greatest cavalry victory of the entire English Civil War.

But again: at what cost, and to what end? There is no record of the royalist losses, perhaps because it is the victors who usually write history, but many suspect those loses were significant. Parliamentarians considered they had suffered far less than they might have done, writing at the time that "we have lost only fifty horse, and at the most two hundred common soldiers slaine, and taken prisoners… no man of note killed or hurt, only Sir Arthur Haselerigge who received a wound in is arme, and an hurt in his eare, but not dangerous: he fought very bravely. We know we killed many of their best men, but not known to us by name, because we lost the field." Waller, as the royalists would find out to their great cost, might have run away - but it was to fight another day.

Historians put the parliamentarian losses at much higher, perhaps 1500, but that includes 1200 soldiers who surrendered. This early in the war they would most likely have been taken prisoner: later on they might well have been massacred. The royalists claimed 600 parliamentarians dead, which you might expect to be an exaggeration, given they also claimed that the parliamentarians were shown as cowards by what their propaganda described as the "battle of Runaway Downe." Perhaps, in those very different times, many of the parliamentarian soldiers simply thought "sod this for a game of soldiers", and returned to wherever they called home.

The royalists again failed to build on victory, and Waller would redeem himself with his New Model Army, a nationwide permanent force with full time soldiers he established in 1645. The New Model Army crushed any royalist uprising in the bud, and Charles, for all his machinations, would lose his head. The English conflict alone saw some 34,000 Parliamentarians and 50,000 Royalists killed in battle, with perhaps another 100,000 dying from the fall out: disease, sieges, food shortages and more. Many more died in Scotland and Ireland. Oh, and one king. To put that in perspective the return of the Black Death from 1664 would kill around 100,000, mainly in London. In return for the losses of a civil war we gained a parliament with teeth, albeit one that was entirely made up of already wealthy and titled men. One of their first acts in 1646 affected Devizes again, as they ordered the castle be demolished. What stands in its place is a Victorian speculative re-imagining, divided into private homes.

Today Roundway Down is one of the most peaceful and beautiful places in Wiltshire, with panoramic views over Bloody Ditch and the site of the old Snob's white horse. If it was not for the information panels you would think this another prehistoric site that has seen nothing more exciting than sheep for thousands of years. From here you can walk to the gallops just before Avebury, and watch racehorses go through their paces. They remind me of another connection to parliament, courtesy of my step mother. Not even moving to rural Wiltshire stopped her from getting the odd modelling job, including one for the Daily Express. The photographer was hysterically camp, with floppy shirt collars and huge flares. The premise for the story was that her family are related to Herbert Jones, who was riding King George V's colt, Anmer, in the 1913 Epsom Derby when suffragette Emily Davison rushed onto the course. Anmer struck her, before rolling over Herbert Jones. Emily Davison died, but Herbert Jones did eventually recover from his injuries. It is not known whether Emily meant to kill herself, or was just trying to attach a suffragette ribbon onto the King's horse as a protest. My step mother has a tea towel that was sold to commemorate the Derby before the race with Herbert Jones clearly shown. When the topic came up at school, our son's teacher was surprised that he knew of the event: amazing what drying up can teach you, and what it took to get women the vote in parliamentary elections.

Alongside the echoes of the Battle of Roundway Down, Oliver's Castle can also play host to another of the mysteries of the Wiltshire countryside. Yes, here be crop circles, and a tale of how our beliefs have changed, because the first recorded one in England was said to be the work of the devil. The Mowing-Devil, a pamphlet published in 1678, promulgated the story of how a Herefordshire farmer, claiming a labourer's price to mow a field of oats was outrageously expensive, said "that the devil should mow it, rather than he". Cue overnight flashing lights and, come daylight, an oval of mown oats. In the 17th century they feared the devil, now it is aliens. Of course it is.

You might guess I am not a believer. Since the early 1970s I have roamed the wheat and barley fields of the Pewsey Vale. Until the first crop circles appeared at the end of that decade nobody ever talked of such a thing. Not our "white witch" Kathleen Wiltshire, not the people who drove the combine harvesters, not us kids who earned pocket money pulling up poppies. From 1975 I cycled home from Devizes to All Cannings – the heart of what is now crop circle country – often late at night and heard and saw nothing. Ditto all the men driving home from the pub in an era when that sort of thing was commonplace.

But I have seen crop circles being made in broad daylight in the middle of the day. On one occasion I was driving a member of the family to see Avebury – he was Californian and convinced the stones were for landing lights – and we happened across a crop circle in progress. I had spotted the two men through a gap in the hedge, and parked where we could peer through to watch them without being seen. String, planks, strange eyepieces on baseball caps, brazenly destroying a farmer's crop in glorious sunshine.

The phenomena has become such an issue that police have asked people to report anyone seen making a crop circle because they can cost a farmer thousands of pounds. At first they were occasional and pretty uninspiring and the novelty of spotting one soon wore off. Then, in July 1990, what has become perhaps the most famous crop circle of all appeared in East Field, Alton Barnes. The 200 metre design arguably took crop circles to a global audience and featured on a Led Zeppelin collection cover. I can remember turning up to see it, parking my motorcycle in a field entrance and then walking past the parked cars on the narrow road up to Milk Hill, each one being ticketed by a pair of policemen. Far below farm owners Tim and Polly Carson were selling refreshments to those wanting to stand in the circle, which seems only fair.

Not far away, by the Barge Inn in Honey Street, there is a new visitor centre dedicated to those fascinated by crop circles. At its opening Tim Carson told the Wiltshire Gazette and Herald that "you get a bit fed up of it. We've had over 120 in the last 25 years. It's not dissimilar to what Banksy does. Some people call it graffiti, he calls it artwork and I suppose the people that do this call this artwork but I call it damage."

Monique Klinkenbergh was involved in curating the visitor centre and, to her credit, the Netherlander runs a website - *cropcircleaccess.com* - that advises on whether access to each new circle has been agreed to by the farmer, and raises funds to compensate for the loss of a crop if they allow visitor access.

"For farmers they are a curse but for researchers and visitors they are a gift," Monique believes, again speaking to the Wiltshire Gazette and Herald, adding that "our inspiration to organise this exhibition is to present more of the unknown facts to the general public to make clear that we are dealing, in some cases, with an authentic, mysterious and misunderstood phenomenon [and] to bring the concerns of the farming community to the attention of the general public and an attempt to find a workable solution to help those farmers who are willing to allow access to visitors who often travelled long distances to Wiltshire to experience the phenomenon."

A believer then. But I will add a caveat to my scepticism. Another farmer nearby told me that he once went out to check on his cattle, around six in the morning, and when he retraced his steps a mist had descended and a crop circle appeared. I know he believes this to be true, and it would be difficult to miss a crop circle. Perhaps the mist made him return to his house a slightly different way and so found the circle he had earlier missed, but I will grant that country folk do not, generally speaking, miss these sort of things.

The visitor centre tells of crop circles throughout history, although I am unconvinced. If I see someone with a new tattoo (usually our daughter) I do not wonder if some mystical event occurred. If a full moon looks unusually big I ask Mr Google why, rather than adopt one of the superstitions of our forefathers. But, as Paul Simon observed in the opening lines of The Boxer, a man hears what he wants to hear - and disregards the rest.

Doug Bower and Dave Chorley admitted they were behind the crop circles in 1991. Initially inspired by stories in Australia that simple circles of fallen wheat might have been landing sites for UFOs, rather than caused by peculiarities in the weather, they wondered if the English might be as prone to flights of fancy. After 200 or so crop circles they decided it was time to come clean. Working with the now defunct *Today* newspaper they made fools of self-proclaimed cereologists (the title crop circle obsessives like to adopt) and even demonstrated that they had adapted their designs to fit in with theories as to how meteorological phenomena might create the circles.

But the cereologists would not be swayed, one telling the *New York Times* that "yesterday there were circles discovered on a prairie in Canada. Have these guys been out there with their board?"

Given that Wiltshire's corn circles were inspired by those in Australia, perhaps Doug and Dave had inspired some Canadians. Or perhaps an alien civilisation that has worked out how to sidestep Albert Einstein's laws of physics really does think the best way to communicate with us is by upsetting farmers and fascinating visitors to Wiltshire. But Tim Carson's comparison with Banksy is fair, and I remember once being told that real art must always be anonymous: to be done for art's sake and not for money or recognition. That is true of the crop circles, and it is a shame farmers cannot turn a loss into a gain. Clearly they cannot drop everything to stand by a gate collecting an entrance fee and, in any event, most crop circles are best seen from the downs. Perhaps a clever copyright lawyer could ensure that each design is the exclusive property of the farmer, although they can usually be photographed from public land and, increasingly, by drones. I feel for both sides: farming is financially perilous as it is, and the loss of thousands of pounds over a few difficult years might be all it takes to finish a family business. And yet, even as a sceptic, I love to catch sight of a new crop circle and appreciate that people come to Wiltshire to see the circles, spending their tourist cash along the way. The police now actively try to catch the circle makers, rightly siding with the farmers over what is an act of vandalism tantamount to theft of the damaged crops. Plainly that is also true of much of what Banksy does, yet the owners of anything he sprays are generally delighted and financially rewarded. It would be nice if the same could be true of crop circles – one in the oil seed rape on Roundway Down this year, incidentally – so that farmers could see them as a benefit rather than uncivil behaviour.

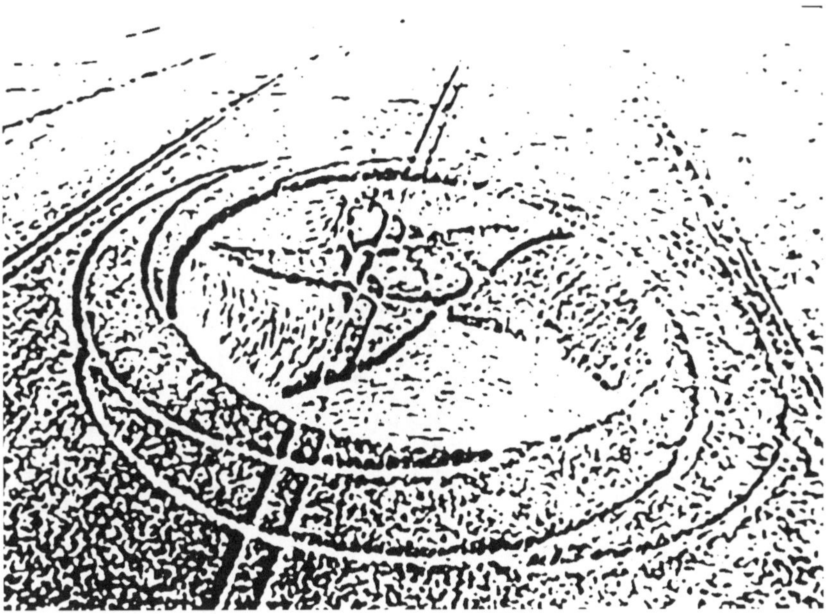

- AUGUST -

SUMMER ON THE LAKES

Astoundingly, tourism generates almost as much income for Wiltshire as it does for Cornwall, and more people actually visit Wiltshire than Cornwall. Admittedly people are often on a short stay on their way to Cornwall, or as part of a tour of England, but the average overseas visitor spends six nights in Wiltshire. So, away from the queues at Stonehenge, where are they all? *Visit Wiltshire* claims that around twenty million people come to the county every year, which is actually more than visit Cornwall. And eighteen million more than visit Stonehenge. Where are they all?

Working in Swindon, I would wager. After all, a visit is not always a holiday, and Swindon is Wiltshire's employment hub. Honda's UK factory is here, drawn by the proximity to London and Bristol's ports. No government incentive was offered or requested: at the time Honda still followed the beliefs of the "Old Man" (the fond nickname for founder Soichiro Honda) that no favours should ever be asked lest they be called in at a later date.

Swindon's policymakers for many years took the view that anyone who brought employment was welcome to set up shop on the wide open plans around the town. Planners elsewhere in the country were appalled, but it had been the attitude that brought Brunel and his GWR workshops to the town. With the switch away from steam in the 1960s, followed by the Beeching cuts and the gradual erosion of the influence of the GWR workshops, decline led to closure in 1986. By then it was employing just 5000 people at a time when Margaret Thatcher's fight against inflation and trade unions was already altering the British economy and employment prospects in a way unimaginable a decade before. Swindon might be a byword for brash business practices, notably spoofed by The Office with David Brent but, having worked there, it is a place for getting things done and not expecting your family tree to be of any help. A meritocracy was rare in market towns, where family and membership of the right organisation got you promoted. In Swindon it was what you had achieved.

So when the gravel pits to the north west of the town were exhausted, not all were left to be nature reserves, even if many are. A scheme was designed to bring back jobs - and to attract tourist and second home owners. With typical brazenness the area was called the Cotswold Water Park, despite being some ten miles from the Cotswold's designated area of outstanding natural beauty (AONB). And, given that most people associate the Cotswold's with honey coloured cottages that have seemingly grown out of the local limestone, saying that a gravel pit is in the Cotswolds is probably pushing your luck a bit too far… and yet.

The thing Wiltshire lacked was always a truly impressive body of water. Yes, we have our two Avons and the chalk streams, but for the most part these are all gentle, quiet affairs. Access to the rivers especially is poor as they cross private farmland for much of their journey. For the most part their routes through towns reflect their value to an industrial past. And any recreational use beyond fishing will upset the fishermen.

But the lakes of north west Wiltshire are very different. Yes, there are spaces for wildlife and quiet contemplation - but there is also a beach, sailing and even water-skiing. The advantage of the lakes being man made is that the layout has been developed to keep conflicting activities apart, and given it is all outside the official AONB building accommodation has not involved conflict with those who think much of England's countryside is perfect and unalterable. Here there are campsites, self catering in Finnish log cabins and so on, all the way up to a luxury spa hotel. Most overlook lakes and, if you want to see the real Cotswolds, in a few minutes you can be driving though the sort of countryside and villages that have probably graced a biscuit tin lid.

One of the most knowledgeable of all English architecture historians, Alex Clifton Taylor, adored the Cotswolds. He had no truck with those (including me, I confess,) who believe them a little repetitive and predictable. In his definitive book, The Pattern of English Building, he wrote lovingly of the quality of the buildings, even the barns.

This might be because the landscape is not especially striking. Certainly at its southern end, down by Bath and Bradford on Avon, there are the occasional packs of closely packed contours, but by and large it is flat to anyone who has lived in the shadow of the chalk downs. That might explain why there are a surprising number of old RAF airfields in the Wiltshire Cotswolds, partly because they were safely out of range to Nazi fighter planes in the Second World War.

But underground, the Cotswolds are fascinating. A geological plan of central and southern Wiltshire is just shades of green, a mix of greensand and chalk, with the odd lens of clay left behind. But travel west, across the fertile clay, and suddenly there is a dizzying variation in the subsoil. You can plot it by looking at the older houses - in the chalk lands only the grandest of buildings are of stone. There is whitewashed cob and chalk, and later brick. But travel west and ever more modest houses are in stone until, as Alex Clifton Taylor observed, eventually even the barns are beautiful stone.

But the availability of stone does not, on its own, allow you to use it for even a modest barn. You must be able to pay for stone to be quarried or mined, dressed and eventually raised into a barn. This was all done, like so much else, on the wealth built from wool - and there was something else in the ground of the Cotswolds that made their sheep farmers even wealthier than their cousins on the chalk: fuller's earth.

Fuller's earth was not discovered by a Mr Fuller, but rather is a clay valued by those who cleaned the wool, reducing oil content and making it thicker along the way. These people were known as fullers. How common they were is told in surnames: they were also known as tuckers or walkers. In times past urine had been used, but then that had to be removed. In any case, fuller's earth made better cloth, and richer farmers who could build their workers prettier villages. They may have been no better than anyone else's inside but that would not stop their master showing off the village to his family and peers from a distance, making him - always a him - look the better man, assured of his place in heaven.

The Cotswolds AONB in Wiltshire as you drive west from the lakes starts just beyond Malmesbury and almost immediately crosses the Fosse Way, the great Roman road that links Exeter on the south west coast of Devon, to Lincoln. A 230 mile (370km) road linking great Roman centres, it was originally a defensive ditch (Fosse means ditch), not unlike the Wansdyke, to defend and mark the north west boundary of the parts of England under Roman control. To the north and west lay the Celts, Scottish and Welsh, that would take more effort to contain and control. Plus the weather was rubbish, especially if you were used to Italy, and the Romans wanted England to be their bread basket, so wanted lands such as Wiltshire where they could readily grow wheat. Bread was the staple food of the Roman empire and as well as improving grain varieties and agricultural efficiency they popularised bread in the English diet. Our damp weather meant building grain dryers that used the famous Roman underground heating to keep mould at bay.

The Romans must have been shocked at how little variety there was in English flora and fauna. When the land bridge to the continent collapsed at the end of the last ice age Britain became as island that kept new species of plants and animals on mainland Europe from reaching us. The Romans brought most of our herbs, chickens, rabbits, hares and much, much more – including leeks. That the Welsh adopted the vegetable as a national symbol is ironic, given that most of Wales had to be contained under military rule while the Romans were here. The relationship in much of England became benign and mutually advantageous: English farmers grew rich selling to the Romans. Having been repelled in 55BC by a combination of Celts and the British weather, Julius Caesar returned a year later with 50,000 troops, more than twice the size of his previous army. They got as far as the Thames – and then left to sort out the Gauls in what we now call France. Oddly, about the only Roman place name that hangs on in England is Britannia – it means the land of tin, something we were trading in prehistory.

That there is no evidence of Roman military encampment in Wiltshire is telling. The first village you reach as you cross the Fosse Way is Easton Royal, probably a hangover from the nearby Roman settlement of Whitewalls. Little of Whitewalls remains other than earthworks, and it has been suggested the Romans just added to an older fort. Others have suggested that the Fosse Way itself pre-dates the Romans. But my oh my, is the Fosse Way straight, a famous Roman trait. The Wansdyke and Ridgeway, by comparison, are not.

Whitewalls – an odd name: perhaps they were built of chalk? – may have started as a fort when the Fosse Way was a defensive line, but it was a small rural town by the time the Romans left Britain. The last Roman left Britain in 410AD, fed up with ever more rebellious barbarians – the Roman word for people from outside their empire – both in Britain and on the mainland.

So, in the words of Monty Python, what did the Romans ever do for us? Less than on the continent, probably. We have no amphitheatres, or spectaculum as the Romans called them. Their successors were farmers, not towns people, so many Roman towns just fell apart. Bradenstoke church, near Royal Wootton Basset, has a huge stone in its base taken from a scavenged nearby Roman villa. The depressions in the ground where Roman buildings have been dismantled are still known as robber's ditches, and some of our sewers are Roman, but there is not the wealth of remains left in France, for example. The Romans made reading and writing more commonplace, making historical research easier. Their legal system has gone, and it left a huge gulf between our system of law and that of, say, France. The French system is codified, meaning that government can strip out a law and it is then as if it had never existed. That was the way with the Romans and Napoleon. In England we could appeal to the monarch, and later a court. English law, and legal systems that followed our path, has a huge number of decided cases now known as equity, originally based on the "keeper of the king's conscience". The decisions in these cases, even when hundreds of years old, are used to judge how statute law – our equivalent of codification – is applied. In theory another Caesar or Napoleon could rise in France and sweep away all laws that did not suit, something that could not happen under English law.

Back in and out of the Cotswolds, generally following the Fosse Way south west to Bath (Aqua Sulis to the Romans), or keeping west and staying within the Cotswolds AONB, the chocolate box villages just keep coming. After Easton Royal is Sherston, one of Alex Clifton-Taylor's favourite villages: more restrained than Castle Combe, and less likely to be overrun with tourists, especially in summer. Then there is the gruesome sounding Slaughterford, probably just from the old English slah-pom, meaning sloe thorn – or it might just be that stones were split to create roofing slates here, especially since a past spelling has been Slatterford. The ford allowed crossing of By Brook. The Romans settled here and Cromwell destroyed the church on his way to fight in Ireland, although it was rebuilt and restored in the nineteenth century.

By the time you get down to Bradford on Avon you realise where all the stone came from, since the old quarries and mine entrances are readily seen. Bath Stone is unusual in that it is typically taken from underground mines rather than from an open quarry. The old mines at Corsham were converted to a top secret underground headquarters for the British Government in the event of a nuclear war. Some 30 metres below beneath Corsham 35 acres of mines were converted during the 1950s to a top secret bunker. Code named Burlington, most of the 4,000 people who would be moved here if nuclear attack was deemed likely had no idea it existed or that they would be expected to abandon family and friends for subterranean offices that stretched for a kilometre. The second biggest telephone exchange in the country and a broadcasting facility for the BBC were just some of the facilities accessed by 60 miles of roads. The facility was considered to be blast proof and able to protect its occupants from the aftermath of a nuclear attack, with enough food and water for at least three months. There is also access to other mines.

In 1991 Burlington was considered to be no longer needed and in 2007 was decommissioned, but these Cold War relics are there if you look for them. Mysterious slip roads on the M4 reputedly gave access to RAF Lyneham, and Devizes old post office was designed by a named architect – KW Judd – rather than the county architects department who designed the contemporary library next door. It turns out a hidden bunker for the great and good of Wiltshire below is the reason.

The work in mines was hard, dangerous and often undertaken in the dark to save candles. Children were expected to be working in some way by the age of five. Women were often back down there the day after giving birth. Little wonder that men were happy to sign up to fight in the First World War, thinking conditions could hardly be worse. Ironically many finished up digging the tunnels that laid mines under enemy positions. The dressed stone (known as ashlar) mined in the Wiltshire Cotswolds may make a romantic backdrop in the regions towns and villages, but getting it out of the ground was fraught with hardship.

The stone buildings of Corsham are another backdrop for period dramas, most recently Poldark. Nick Mason of Pink Floyd fame is also a resident. Wiltshire's emptiness, so close to London, does seem to attract pop stars: Sting, Madonna and Robbie Williams are others who have made the country their home.

Back in Bradford on Avon there is another piece of wartime history. Below quarrymen's homes, Upper Westwood quarry is accessed via a long tunnel, its stone flecked with rusty patches, still occasionally extracted when a match to an old building is needed. Otherwise it is now largely used for secure storage but, during the Second World War, it was a factory for making gun sights by Royal Enfield and for storing the treasures of the British and the Victoria & Albert Museums.

In June 1941 Royal Enfield moved from Redditch in Worcestershire to avoid being destroyed by a bombing raid of the sort that had razed Coventry the previous year. Ironically Bradford on Avon became a more likely site for German bombs when Joseph Goebbels ordered the Luftwaffe to divert their Blitzes to English cities featured in a famous German tourist guide, the *Baedeker*.

In 1942 the Royal Air Force completely revised its bombing strategy, using bigger aircraft to attack clusters of strategic targets. There was also a change of attitude towards destroying civilian towns and cities in the belief that this would hurt morale and weaken the German people's admiration of Hitler. One of our old neighbours had been a navigator on an RAF bomber that attacked Dresden, the nadir of this strategy and, even in his seventies, still regretted his part in that night's raids. But the first casualty had been the historic town of Lübeck on 28 to 29 March 1942. Goebbels opened his copy of the *Baedeker* and started with Exeter, at the far end of the Fosse Way, and Bath a few miles from Bradford on Avon on the night of 25-26 April.

What Goebbels did not know was that the RAF had aircraft with their own radar, successfully developed as night fighters. The Bristol Beaufighter night fighters were regularly based at RAF Colerne in the Wiltshire Cotswolds, for example, which was almost on the flightpath of Goebell's bombers. The Beaufighters had what looked a little like a pair of garden forks sticking out from their nosecones, although these were fastidiously removed from photographs lest the Germans guess the aircraft had radar. To explain away the success that the RAF had bringing down enemy bombers in a dark, moonless sky, the public were told that the pilots existed on a diet of carrots, carrots and more carrots. There is some truth that carrots might help a little with eyesight, but the story was pure propaganda. Radar, as in the Battle of Britain, was our secret weapon.

At the end of the war Royal Enfield seemingly forgot to leave Westwood Quarry. Their outbuildings were cleared for housing, so remaining underground was really the only option. Post war they resumed production of a range of single cylinder motorcycles, similar to the type now made in India and exported all over the world. After the Second World War all English manufacturing industries were implored to "export or die", especially to the United States, really the only sizeable market place not still reeling from the after effects of the war. But the Americans liked big, fast twin cylinder motorcycles designed for their straight roads and huge distances. Royal Enfield's answer was the Interceptor, with 736cc and 53bhp making it one of the fastest production motorcycles on earth. Richard Stevens, who still runs a motorcycle dealership in Devizes, was the test and development rider.

"I was told to ride out of the tunnel quietly, but could never resist giving it some welly. The sound coming off the walls sounded fantastic to me, but apparently I was deafening back in the old mine. I got some bollockings, but they were worth it."

Richard raced and won for Royal Enfield, partly for the joy and partly to develop the bike. When Royal Enfield folded in 1968 Richard was working on an 800 Interceptor he wound up to 128mph at the Motor Industries Research Association's testing facilities in Warwickshire. "It was the best time of my life" Richard smiles, but it was to no avail. British management did not see the Japanese as a threat, believing they were growing the market with small capacity motorcycles whose riders would soon move up to bigger, English, machines. 1968 was the year Honda revealed its seminal CB750 with four cylinders, an electric starter, disc front brake and unquestioned reliability. The best selling motorcycle magazine in the world, *Cycle* in the US, called it "the most sophisticated production bike ever". Within a decade the British motorcycle industry was gone.

The Japanese, along with the Chinese, taught us that most English of summer ceremonies: afternoon tea. Both countries were closed when we went Empire building and the Dutch beat us to it anyway. Luckily for British ambitions the Dutch economy imploded when people realised tulip bulbs had no intrinsic value, but it took war and a deliberate campaign to get the Chinese addicted to opium before we had their secrets of manufacturing fine porcelain - which many people still call china. The English discovered tea bushes would grow just as well in the mountains of India as in the Orient, saving us the trouble of dealing with people who wanted nothing to do with outsiders.

The English love of tea led to the first use of computers in our private sector: pretty much in the world, in fact. J Lyons & Co sold a quarter of the tea bought in Britain post war, and ran a chain of some 200 tea shops. This was a huge logistical operation and to make it work so, in October 1947, the company decided to build their own digital computer. Initially this was to manage their own product distribution, but with an eye on selling large scale computers to other business. This was despite Thomas Watson, president of IBM, predicting in 1943 that he thought "there is a world market for maybe five computers".

In 1951 the first Lyons Electronic Office (LEO – see what they did there?) booted up, its 3,000 electronic valves able to run 650 instructions a second – less than a third of the power of an iPad. But LEO filled a large room, and it was the need for plenty of space - and a space with a carefully controlled environment - that led Thomas Watson to doubt the demand for computers.

Although LEO cost Lyons £100,000 it saved the company that much within two years. Everybody beat a path to Lyons' doors, from city brokers, to the Ford motor company, to the military on both sides of the Iron Curtain. The first big MoD computer based in Britain was Bureau West, in what was then open countryside north of Devizes. Opened in 1976, I remember a school visit. We were warned we might need coats, because computers like to be cool: your iPhone might be fine at room temperature, but Facebook servers are up by the Arctic Circle.

Inside Bureau West was like a 1960 James Bond film: big spools running ticker tape, hushed men in lab coats, cooling air blowing used ticker tape around. We were told that all that was done here was the MoD payroll, but questions about overnight security were asked in Parliament – appropriate given that the site of the battle of Roundway Down is easily seen from Bureau West.

LEO was incorporated into the British Government backed ICL (International Computers Limited), a competitor to Americas IBM. There was much controversy when Bureau West was announced, with IBM a front runner to provide the computers, although ICL won in the end. And, despite what we were told on our school trip, there was never an official announcement as to what those computers were for.

Such is the world of computing, Bureau West only lasted until 1983 and is now a housing estate. But it is still a matter of record that an English tea company was at the forefront of our military's computer technology.

You can still recreate the earliest English experiences of tea drinking in Wiltshire. Just north of Salisbury there is a Japanese garden in the grounds of Heale house, and just south of the Cotswolds is Beggars Knoll Chinese Garden, at Newtown near Westbury.

If you have cause to wonder why August has that still air when the weather plays ball, it is because there is no birdsong. With mating and fledging over, the birds need to moult, which makes flying tricky or, in some species, impossible. So the birds keep quiet, hiding from predators until they are back in their full feathered finery, and to allow us a perfect slice of a silent English summer. It will make a change from following the tourists, but if you visit Beggars Knoll, occasionally open under the National Gardens Scheme (the so called "Yellow Book" gardens, because of the colour of the guide) and then Heale you can drive back up across the plains and downs of Wiltshire to spend what is left of summer on the lakes.

- SEPTEMBER -

OH, WHAT A NIGHT

Wool might have made Wiltshire – along with most of Britain – rich, but from around 1830 demand started to wane, and another cash cow was desperately needed. The reasons for the decline in demand for wool and cloth are not immediately obvious, but imports from the Empire and competition from the huge industrialised mills in Yorkshire could not have helped. Wiltshire had not been slow to embrace new technology – Trowbridge had a steam engine powered mill in 1805 – but the focus remained on high quality cloth. In contrast, demand from an increasingly urban population was for the latest fashion at ever cheaper prices. Sounds familiar?

And what an increasing population. In the first ever census, in 1801, the population of England stood at well under eight million. Over the next century more than that number left our shores for empire, either to seek their fortune, to work or transported by the courts. Yet the 1901 census recorded over 30 million souls living in England, mostly in towns and cities.

Fortunately for Wiltshire's farmers Brunel's new railway meant that fresh milk could be sold into London, and the sheep of the country were rapidly replaced by cattle: genuinely cash cows, which could fertilise the fields while producing milk and meat. Better yet, cows do not graze meadowland as closely as sheep, so it was possible to rotate the livestock whilst fertilising the fields, ready to sow wheat. Wheat was still incredibly lucrative, largely because of the Corn Laws from 1815. Wealthy landowners did not appreciate being undercut by cheap imports, so set about introducing a minimum price for corn. Bread prices rocketed, and with so many more mouths to feed tempers of ordinary people started to fray. Not only were jobs being lost in the cloth industry, farm workers' winter pay was evaporating. Traditionally a big part of this was threshing, working in barns to separate the wheat from the chaff. But the new threshing machines made this work redundant, to the delight of farmers who had a guaranteed price for their corn alongside a lower wage bill. What could go wrong?

In the previous century the so called Luddites had threatened anyone installing new technology that would reduce the need for workers with letters from General or King Ludd, an invented persona that gave the protesters an anonymous leader. The owners of new threshing machines were now receiving similar threats signed by the fictional Captain Swing, giving a label to the Swing riots of 1830.

Bishopdown Farm, near Salisbury, was the site of a Swing riot on 23 November 1830, when a small army destroyed a threshing machine and then marched on to Salisbury with a view to meting out a similar fate to Figes' iron foundry. The wealthy fled with what they could carry: in those days there was no police force to call, just a parish constable. Despite the Riot Act of 1714 allowing a local authority to declare a group of a dozen or more men an unlawful assembly and demand they disperse, in practice there was little one man with a stone lock up – the so called blind rooms – could do.

The Salisbury attack was headed off by a hastily assembled militia, but it was clear that the divide in society needed to be healed. Farmers were becoming gentlemen, requiring their ever fewer workers to live outside the farmhouse, and in the towns factory workers lived away from the wealthier quarters. Pushing the poor into one place might have seemed a good idea, but it meant they could compare notes and grudges, and decide what to do about it. By 1836 this had led to the Chartists, a group which laid out six demands to Parliament: the vote for all men over 21; that it would be a secret ballot; an MP need not be a landowner; MPs should be salaried; electoral districts should be of equal size; and Parliamentary elections should be an annual event.

In other words, the Chartists wanted an ordinary working man to have the opportunity to be an MP, and that his peers might vote for him. Reasonable enough now, but at the time Parliament was effectively solely the House of Lords. And yet there was sympathy for the uprisings: William Cobbett, a farmer, journalist and MP protested that too many of his peers had come to treat farm workers as "real slaves". There was a mood in the country that perhaps it was time for another civil war.

One man, Prime Minister Sir Robert Peel, led the resolution. In 1846 he succeeded in leading a Parliamentary repeal of the Corn Laws, but his lasting legacy is of course his Bobbies – a permanent police force. The 1829 Metropolitan Police Bill gave London a police force, and by 1836 Salisbury had followed suit. Just three years later the Wiltshire Police force was born but, given that most people had no say in how they were ruled, life remained harsh for all but the fortunate few. That a police force was needed is reminded by a stone on the Devizes to Salisbury Road: it commemorates the spot where a farmer was held up by four men on October 21st 1839. Fighting back from his carriage with a whip he shouted for "George! George!" even though he knew he was alone. The highwaymen were convinced he had help at hand, however, and fled. But the farmer pursued them for three hours, when one of the would be thieves collapsed and died. There is a second stone at this spot on Chapperton Down, and both stones are inscribed with reminders of the day, and that the three highwaymen who initially escaped were captured and transported. Paid for by public subscription, this was very much community policing in the year Wiltshire's formal police force was formed. And although dealing with highwaymen and robbers was very much part of the force's remit, concern about the Chartists was also a large part of the wealthy being prepared to pay taxes that might protect the status quo.

So much is written and taught in our schools – quite rightly – on female suffrage that it is easy to forget that the vast majority of men were similarly denied the vote. This was still true when, as we saw earlier, Emily Davison was killed in her protest at the 1913 Epsom Derby. Suffrage – from the Latin, meaning to vote – was denied to any man without certain property rights until 1918. Gradually the right to vote was extended, largely in the hope of keeping the revolutions affecting mainland Europe from English shores. But Lord Palmerston summed up the thoughts of his (literally) peers in 1864 when he wrote to the prime minister, a fellow Lord - Gladstone - saying: "I deny that every sane and not disqualified man has a moral right to vote. What every man and woman too have a right to, is to be well governed and under just laws". In other words, ruled by clever people like us. Because intelligence is about inherited wealth and titles.

But Palmerston died soon afterwards, and his replacement Lord Derby, fearful of revolution and trying to prop up a weakened Conservative Party, introduced the 1867 Reform Act. This doubled the number of men eligible to vote, and meant Devizes ceased to be represented by two MPs, a privilege it had always enjoyed apart from the period of unpleasantness during the English Civil War. Gradually the system became fairer, votes being anonymous to minimise the risk of corruption and coercion, constituencies being more representative of the number of voters living there. But the real reform came as a result of the First World War and the 1916 Military Service Act passed into law that every British man between 18 and 41 was "deemed to have enlisted" in the army. Conscription sent men who had no say in how their country was run to be killed in their hundreds and thousands and injured in their millions.

The 1918 Representation of the People Act granted a vote to women over the age of 30 who met a property qualification. Not ideal, but a start that would take a decade to put women on an equal footing with men. The Act gave the vote to all men over the age of 21. The bill was passed in the House of Commons by 385 votes in favour to 55 against, and in 1928 the Act was extended to allow all women over 21 to be allowed to vote. 713 years after King John had signed the Magna Carta we finally had a true democracy.

Proposing the changes in 1918 the home secretary George Cave remarked that: "War by all classes of our countrymen has brought us nearer together, has opened men's eyes, and removed misunderstandings on all sides. It has made it, I think, impossible that ever again, at all events in the lifetime of the present generation, there should be a revival of the old class feeling which was responsible for so much, and, among other things, for the exclusion for a period, of so many of our population from the class of electors. I think I need say no more to justify this extension of the franchise."

The Devizes MP welcomed the change. Lieutenant Colonel Cory Heward was a British Army officer born in Seend, in Wiltshire. He fought in the Boer and both World Wars, surviving them all. The family home, Cleeve House, was built with the profits of Welsh coalmines, but it sits on a ridge overlooking an almost endless expanse of fertile farmland that runs to the far off Downs and the Ridgeway. Heward would have watched the harvests being gathered in. Wheat and barley would still have been harvested with a scythe in his time: although horse drawn reapers had been around since around 1830, people were cheap to hire, especially the travelling labourers. A good worker was expected to clear a quarter of an acre a day when five acres was a big field. Regardless of how it was cut the wheat would have been gathered up in stooks that looked like small wigwams. This allowed the wheat to start the drying process.

There was usually a sense of party during the wheat harvest, along with a sense of urgency. The "harvest moon" is the full moon closest to the autumn equinox, valuable to allow extra light to work by if getting the harvest in is running late. It may look bigger than other full moons, but that is an optical illusion caused by it being close to the horizon: it is the same reason a harvest moon can have a red or orange tinge.

The cutting down of the final sheaf of corn was steeped in tradition. Known as the nack, taking it down required a particular – knack. Pagan beliefs held firm that some spirit of the harvest would have retreated into this final cut, and it might have been cut by an elected harvest king, or by throwing scythes at it. Eventually the sheaf would be spared the stook, decorated to celebrate the harvest and the stalks turned into corn dollies. These would be buried when the next year's crop was sown, ensuring continued fertility.

With the nack sorted out, the gleaners were allowed onto the field to collect the spilt and abandoned grains before the crows, rooks and pigeons moved in. In *The Folklore of Wiltshire* Ralph Whitlock writes that the traditional communal cry at the end of the harvest in Wiltshire ran: "Well ploughed! Well sowed! Well harrowed! Well mowed! All safely carted to the barn with nary a load throwed! Hip hip hip hooray!" – in other words it was time to party.

Ralph Whitlock writes that the golden years of the harvest supper were during the second half of the nineteenth century but that they had pretty much gone by 1900. The suppers seem to have been quite lavish - or at least they seemed so to the farm workers who attended them. Food was plentiful, and drink was even more so. A cornet player at one supper was claimed to have asked that someone "prop I up somewhere so's I can't vall over and I'll keep playing for ee."

Contrary to common myth, beer was not drunk as an alternative to fresh water to avoid disease, certainly not in the countryside.

Wiltshire's chalk streams and springs where the chalk meets the greensand would have provided plenty of good quality drinking water. What beer provided was calories, perhaps as many as a third of the calories taken in by a medieval labourer. It is a measure of how mollycoddled we are that it is recommended that a man takes in no more than 2,500 calories a day. When I mentioned to my brother in law – a Royal Marine – that a medieval labourer needed more like 6,000 calories a day his ears pricked up: that is the calorie count of some Special Forces daily ration pack. Beer provided it, and small beer – made from the third mash, so the cheapest available – was also not very alcoholic. We think – the varieties used back then are different to those we now harvest. But almost certainly well under one per cent proof, and yes, drunk by small boys – small beer. Something much stronger would have been drunk at celebrations. Brewed in Devizes, Wadworth's famous 6X was originally 6% proof – an X was branded onto a barrel for every per cent of alcohol, so small beer had just the one X. Rationing in the Second World War reduced it to 4.2% and it never recovered. But during the harvest suppers fairs and carnivals 6% alcohol by volume would have been typical for a beer, with cider stronger still. Wine was unaffordable to agricultural workers.

I can still remember the drive over to Pewsey for the last carnival of the year, carnivals that have grown out of the parties that marked the end of the harvest. Because it was so late in the year even allowing for a youngster's bedtime the journey across the Pewsey Vale was in the dark, wowed by the fields on fire. It was outlawed for environmental reasons, but in the 1970s the stubble was dealt with by setting fire to it, and it was a remarkable sight. Acres literally ablaze, lighting up the night under a harvest moon.

Although the word carnival derives from the Latin for "the meat goes", a celebration before lent at the end of winter, such a Catholic habit had disappeared in England during the reformation. After all, we had refused to adopt the Gregorian calendar that much of Europe switched to in 1582 as it was seen to be too Popish. But eventually the drift of the seasons became impossible to ignore and England succumbed to the Gregorian calendar in 1751. Its introduction was not straightforward. It meant that 1751 lasted just 282 days, starting on the Julian calendar's new year: the 25th March.

1752 then began on 1 January, but we found ourselves still adrift of many European calendars by 11 days. So Wednesday the 2nd September 1752 was followed by Thursday 14th September, leading to unrest and people believing their lives had just been foreshortened. It was still a matter of dispute in the 1754 election campaign, as saints' days and other traditional markers were shuffled around the calendar. For instance some believe that Samhain or Old Winter's Day was on the 11th October and appropriated by the church as Michaelmas, now on the 29th September, although most think that Samhain was on 31st October and is the basis of Hallowe'en.

St Michael is the archangel who drove Satan from Heaven, and it said that blackberries must not be picked after his saints' day because they will be spoilt by the devil's spit: it is true that around this time they start to go over and rot. But 29th September would become the day of the hiring fairs, the day one agricultural year ended and a new one began.

It could also cause confusion in Wiltshire, where land had traditionally changed hands on Lady Day, the 25th March and once the first day of the year. If the land had the previous tenant's crops on it there was nothing could be done until Michaelmas. On the other hand there might be a late root crop to compensate, and it was not as if farmers had plenty of spare time.

Michaelmas would be the time of England's carnivals, the party at the end of harvest, revelry that would go on for days. There would be a carnival queen, games in the streets and a lantern parade. Wiltshire is full of them, modern lorries dressed up by local businesses, charities and social groups with a humorous theme, music and lighting. Carnival events might include a confetti battle, good naturedly fought on the streets of market towns and – of course – a fun fair.

But these carnivals had a serious purpose, first served by the Hiring or "Mop" fairs, one of which hangs on in Marlborough although you would struggle to distinguish it from other local carnivals. Brought in by Edward III, trying to address the desperate shortage of labour caused by the Black Death. Labourers on the lookout for a new employer, and vice versa, prospective employees holding or wearing something that hinted at the type of work they could do. The lowest cleaners would carry a mop, or just some cloth loops from a mop head on their lapel. The most respected trade, the shepherd need just to carry his crook. The mop fairs did get a reputation for overindulgence and immorality over time, a tradition that modern carnivals thankfully continue. After all, if you have had to work hard, making hay while the sun shone, it is only fair that you play hard when the sun goes down.

Of course wheat, barley and oats were not the only harvests. Wheat was the last arable crop to come in, but hay making would have started in June. But these were the important harvests, the ones that would allow you to be sure you had beer and bread, and that the livestock could survive the winter. Root vegetables might still be in the ground, especially in the well drained greensand that covers much of Wiltshire. The apple harvest, essential for cider, might run on until December, depending on the variety and how quickly winter bares her claws. And then there is the "blood harvest", when the decision is made on which livestock will be kept for next spring, and which is to be winter's larder.

One of the things that makes Ralph Whitlock's *Folklore of Wiltshire* such a fine and credible book is that his father was a pig slaughterer and that Ralph regularly travelled with him. The cost was two shillings and sixpence for each slaughter - about £8 in today's money. At that price Mr Whitlock senior expected to keep the offal, either for himself or to sell on. Offal – the edible internal organs and entrails – do not keep well and in those pre-freezer days needed to be processed quickly and eaten fairly soon.

Although there are tales of killing pigs with a nail hammered into the skull, the usual method was to slit the throat and drain the carcass as quickly as possible to keep the parts that could be cured as fresh as possible. The blood, with oats, would make black pudding. You can still see the hatches on the outside of many cottages chimneys where the bacon would be smoked. In parts of England a side – flitch – of bacon would be given to newlyweds who had shown the greatest devotion, thus able to bring home the bacon. Geoffrey Chaucer laments in *The Wife of Bath's Tale* "but never for us the flitch of bacon".

Famously only the pig's squeak is wasted. The bladder would become a football, and a game would be played between villages. Football did not grow, like so many English sports, from the public schools, but from the celebration of the coming feasting that might follow the slaughter of a pig. There are records of football matches with over a hundred players. The reason the modern game has 11 players is simply because that is the number in a cricket team. As football became a sport that might earn players a living, cricket teams – who had no means of earning outside the cricket season – became football players as well.

In Wiltshire it was believed that pigs had to be killed on a waxing moon or the meat would go bad, although Ralph Whitlock's father thought it mere superstition. But until quite recently pigs were a small part of farming, more usually a porker kept in the back garden fed on leftovers. A fully grown pig has a carnivores' ability to bite, so keeping them in numbers was strictly for the brave and even tempered. Pigs love company and are affectionate creatures – but not to be messed with.

They also seem to have a sense of humour. The aptly named Butcher family kept them at the northern edge of the village I grew up in and, inevitably, they would occasionally escape. Viewed from the safety of my bedroom window a handful of pigs would run in one direction, pursued by the Butcher boys. And then, apparently deciding they missed their home would run back towards the sties, chased by the ever more ruddy faced Butchers. We may only have had three television channels, but there was plenty to watch.

The biggest decision of all in livestock farming falls to the shepherd. While artificial insemination is now routine in large cattle herds, a flock of sheep is a dynamic, long lived organism. Keeping the best rams is essential to the long term health of the flock, but most of this year's crop need to go to market to pay the farmer. Some of these sheep fairs could see 100,000 animals change hands – wheat and cattle might have been bigger cash generators by 1900, but sheep farming was still huge- although as we saw earlier, you cannot have an English lamb at Easter, because a lamb is a creature slaughtered before their first birthday. The ram that is lucky enough to be kept was traditionally tupped – put out to mate - with his ewes on Guy Fawkes night with a view to lambs arriving on April fool's day. If Easter is early, it will have already been and gone by then.

By the end of September the weather has usually become settled although, paradoxically, this is also a month when high winds and storms are possible. But the sunlight is very distinctive, reminiscent of the golden hours at the beginning and end of the day in summer. The beauty is ramped up by the colour of the leaves, due to chlorophyll returning to the tree and allowing the true colours of deciduous leaves to shine. As someone who has suffered from depression, I find it strangely wonderful and dreadful at once – the countryside is as beautiful as it gets, but winter is obviously on the way. It is most keenly felt on a late September morning, letting the chickens out. Perhaps it is the memories of the earlier morning of the first day back at school, realising you have been sleeping though the cooling and darkening dawn. A clear September day with leaves starting to turn gold is beautiful, but it is hard to forget that winter is on the way and that the best of the year is behind us.

Especially at the A'Beckett vineyard at Littleton Panel, about to start harvest. They overcame a hard, late frost that did for all our plums and most of our pears, but vines are robust little beggars. My brother and his wife helped out with picking grapes that will finish up as a rose wine made with a mix of a German white grape and the red pinot noir. Like our ancestors we prepare for winter, even if supermarkets mean we do not have to. The dog avoids the overpowering smell of vinegar in the kitchen while I boil down the figs that never ripened for chutney. Apple jelly that goes fabulously with chicken liver pate, and quince jelly for cheese, known as marmelada in Portugal: probably where we get our word marmalade from, the stuff that paid for Keiller's archaeological investigations at Avebury. A harvests of a different sort and the tying up of threads at the end of the farming year.

Traditionally land would now have been ploughed and left for winter frosts to rid of disease and break to soil into something ready to turn into a seedbed next year. Dark nights would be just that, with little respite. No wonder the mop fairs, carnivals and harvest suppers were so loved: from now in the only warmth is from the firewood that has been gathered and dried, and from food that becomes increasing hearty. Once Michaelmas is over, if you are not ready for winter, you might not see spring. And what harm a celebration when you have months to recover. No wonder October arrived with so many waking up and saying, "Oh, what a night!"

- OCTOBER -

FLIGHTS OF FANCY

It would have been around October 1969, sitting in the classroom of our school in the Pewsey Vale, when a low groan from outside rapidly became a crescendo. Either King Kong was out there, clearing his throat, or…

All the boys fell silent and stared at the headmaster, with pleading eyes. Mr Ash smiled, raised both hands and said: "Into the playground". We ran.

Concorde flew almost directly above us, a thing of such dazzling beauty, in a world where the most complex machine I had seen in the flesh was a combine harvester, that I could not speak. Right there my obsession with the Apollo missions died – Neil Armstrong, Buzz Aldrin and Michael Collins had been to the moon a few months earlier, landing Armstrong and Aldrin on its surface. And no, I did not have to look Michael Collins' name up, even after all these years. Until the motorcycle obsession kicked in during 1975, military aircraft would be all I could draw, think of and read about. I joined the Air Training Corps (ATC) six months before I was the 13 years and nine months required, because Devizes (2385 detached flight, later 2397 squadron) was newly formed and desperate for recruits. Before I was much older I was air experience flying in the back of a de Havilland Chipmunk at Filton airfield, now sadly gone. And there, parked insouciantly, in the way friends would later park a new motorcycle outside a pub, not having breathed a word that they were going up in the world, was Concorde. Did we want to look inside?

Actually it was a disappointment. It was tiny, not helped by being rammed full of what looked like `fridge freezers installed by an electrician being paid on the basis of how much wire he could use. The windows were tiny. But it was Concorde, the world's first supersonic airliner.

Or was it, we speculated? It was now autumn 1973, and Concorde's stock had fallen disastrously. After an initial flurry of orders, Concorde was almost immediately banned from the USA, officially on noise grounds, but more likely because John F Kennedy had announced America would develop something faster and bigger. It took until 1977 for the US courts to throw out the ban, but by then it hardly mattered. The Boeing 747 had killed Concorde, as well as the British seaside holiday. Yes, Concorde could reach New York an hour and a half before it left London on local times. But the 747 could offer either much, much cheaper flights or fabulous luxury in first class.

Yet Britain and France struggled on with Concorde, despite not even being able to agree how to spell the name although, eventually, the French got their final "e". A world tour ended with more orders being cancelled than agreed, as the effect of the sonic boom and the black soot from the engines - which were derived from military applications - gave the nascent environmentalists cause to press pause.

Those of us in the ATC had a theory about this. The V-bombers that formed our nuclear deterrent were long in the tooth and were not even supersonic, while Concorde could comfortably reach Mach two – twice the speed of sound. Surely it would soon fly with RAF roundels? Sadly, no. But still I was smitten, even though it was years before I realised the story of military air power started in Wiltshire.

On 16 October 1908 the first accepted flight of a powered aircraft in Great Britain was claimed by a larger than life – aren't they all? – American who had taken the name Samuel Franklin Cody, hoping he would be taken as a descendent of Buffalo Bill Cody. His aircraft, designated Army Aeroplane No1, was a biplane similar to the Wright brothers'. Cody managed just 1,390 feet (424m), crashing as he tried to avoid trees and clipped a wingtip on the ground. But he had proved a point, and the United Kingdom was about to gain an air force.

Within a year Horatio Barber was renting land at Lark Hill, within sight of Stonehenge. He built a shed – the word hanger came later - to house his new aircraft. Barber had made his fortune in Canadian silver mines and a New York Casino, and brought together aeronautical engineers William Manning and Howard Wright to form Aeronautical Syndicate Ltd (ASL). Setting up shop at Lark Hill they were soon joined by like minded souls, including Captain John Fulton who served with the artillery. Training the artillery was one of the main reasons the War office had started buying up Salisbury Plain in 1897, and experimenting with balloons to guide ordinance. People such as Fulton were quick to recognise the advantage of a powered aircraft over a tethered balloon and Lark Hill became home to Larkhill, the army camp, in 1910. But the war office initially believed the future lay with airships, their size allowing them to carry wireless telegraphs that could instantly transmit the position of enemy troops and potential targets. Such was this prejudice that when a pilot landed and telephoned in his report during an exercise the umpire discounted his contribution, insisting he would have been shot dead.

Yet others truly believed aeroplanes were the future of war. In 1908 HG Wells' novel *War in the Air* was published, predicting precisely what would come to pass. Critics were horrified at the idea of a future where a country would reign down death and terror on a neighbouring states' civilian population from flying machines. Many claimed it could never come to pass, officers being gentlemen and so on, but fortunately others realised it was only too likely to be the way of future wars and that our army needed aeroplanes and pilots.

One of these people was Charles Rolls, of Rolls Royce fame. He offered to train pilots for the army and, in October 1909, the war office started looking for a suitable airfield to support Rolls' project. *The Aero* magazine had declared "Salisbury Plain the best stretch of country in England for the training of aviators", and soon there were army aircraft sheds next to those of ASL: comically the Ordinance Survey maps originally marked these as "flying sheds", soon amended to "aeroplane sheds".

Horatio Barber realised his ASL business was not large enough to compete with Britain's rapidly evolving aircraft industry and sold his shed to the British and Colonial Aeroplane Company, a forerunner of British Aerospace. They were joined by the No2 Company of the Air Battalion Royal Engineers, the first flying unit of the armed forces to use powered aircraft. What remains of the hangars are now Grade II* listed: the switch to calling them hangars rather than sheds probably came during the First World War, adopting the word the French used for the large canvas structures aircraft were stored in. After all, they were more like a marquee than a shed.

(A listed building is one on the statutory List of Buildings of Special Architectural or Historic Interest. This gives them a protection from unauthorised change or demolition. Most are Listed Grade II, and only the most important are Grade II* or Grade I)

There were also now aeroplanes with wireless telegraphs. A pilot would have to tap out Morse code with one hand while holding the control column in the other. But then one of the assessments for suitability as a pilot was called "head in bag', with an observer covering the recruit's head "for not less than nine minutes on each course… pilot must not deviate more than 15 degrees off his course at any one time." Nor, presumably, tap out SOS while having a panic attack.

Early aviators faced terrible danger. The aircraft were fragile and difficult to fly, especially as you often had to teach yourself. Pilots had yet to realise an aircraft needed to bank in a turn if it was to remain stable, so fought to keep the wings horizontal, turning the way you would in a car. Despite motorcycle riders proving the benefit of leaning into a turn, pilots resisted an aircraft's wish to do the same causing them to lose height and sometimes control. Charles Rolls was the first British aviation fatality, killed in a crash at the Bournemouth Gymkhana on 12 July 1910, before he could teach any army flyers. 1912 gave the junction by Stonehenge its name, Airman's Cross. Many see the road sign and assume it refers to the road layout, but the memorial by the Stonehenge visitors centre tells that this was the spot of the Royal Flying Corps' first fatal aeroplane crash. Captain Eustace Loraine and his observer, Staff Sergeant (although at least one newspaper reported Sergeant Major) Richard Wilson died here shortly after taking off from Larkhill.

The next month the first military aeroplane trials were held at Larkhill, testing aircraft that included the Avro Type G and the Bristol Gordon England biplane, but the competition was won by Samuel Franklin Cody in his latest prototype. In 1911 the war office converted the Balloon Section of the Royal Engineers into an air force, basing its No2 Company, equipped with aeroplanes, at Larkhill. In 1912 the company became part of the newly formed Royal Flying Corps (RFC). The Larkhill aerodrome was closed in 1914 as the units were dispatched to France but the Listed hangers and memorial are still easily found. The old water tower for the subsequent Stonehenge airfield a few miles to the south of Lark Hill on the eastern side of the A360 road to Salisbury is also clearly visible: this was at the southern end of the Larkhill light railway that served the camp from 1902 and was much expanded over the following years, all the way down past the Handley Page bomber hangers and to the airfield itself. It is possible to walk many of the old railway line routes, marvelling at the sheer number of apple trees in the hedges, where troops discarded cores. Some of the rail track is now kerbing in Shrewton, apparently installed by villagers fed up with American tanks damaging pavements as they prepared for D-Day.

How rapidly aircraft were improving in the run up to the First World War was demonstrated during the Daily Mail Circuit of Britain Air Race in July 1911. Less than eight years previously, on December 17 1903, Orville Wright made the first powered flight in history, travelling just 120 feet (36.5m): less than the wingspan of a Boeing 747. The Circuit of Britain was a 1,010 mile race with 13 staging posts: starting at the new Brooklands racing circuit in Surrey, a short first hop to RAF Hendon allowed for the real racing to start. From here it was on to Harrogate with 150,000 spectators, then Newcastle, Edinburgh, Stirling and Glasgow. From here the race headed south to Carlisle, Manchester, Bristol and Exeter. Then, in recognition of its place in aviation history, the competitors few on to a stop at Larkhill before flying to Brighton and the finishing line back at Brooklands.

The race was won by Jean Conneau, a French navy Lieutenant, entered (as seemed normal practice) under a pseudonym as André Beaumont. His prize was £10,000, equivalent to over a million pounds today. His winning margin was almost two hours, with a total flying time of 23 hours 38 minutes. His average speed of less than 43mph might not impress us now, but it was ground breaking in 1911, especially as war increasingly seemed inevitable.

That the war office was happy to put its new airfield so close to Stonehenge, and test new aircraft designs by flying over it might tell how little we once cared for these old stones. Yet the local planning authority insisted that the sheds did not obscure the view from Stonehenge of the sun rising on the summer solstice, so even by 1910 there were locals concerned with protecting our heritage.

But there is a huge upside to the RFC's time at Stonehenge – photographs of the stones. The purpose of early military aircraft was to take photographs to help the artillery identify and hit targets. It would be well into the First World War before aircraft were armed. Initially German and British aviators would wave at each other, despite knowing the other was working to kill his fellow countryman. It is not known who first thought to take a pot shot at an enemy aircraft but, once the idea had taken hold, we were quickly on the way to designing fighter aircraft to protect reconnaissance machines. And then, rather than photograph a target, why not just drop bombs on it while you are there? Aerial warfare was with us, and HG Wells' predictions had proved correct.

When the Germans began bombing the British mainland, the war office decided they needed to be able to reciprocate. Turning the Stonehenge site into a full blown military airfield began in 1917, officially opening in November. Initially for training, from January 1918 it became the No 1 school of aerial navigation and "bomb dropping". The Royal Naval Air Service (RNAS) Handley Page bombers flew in to an airfield and hangers south of Stonehenge and what is now the A303 at the beginning of 1918. The accomodation for the airfield was mainly immediately west of the stones. This aerodrome would soon be part of a new independent air force, the first in the world, when the Royal Air Force (RAF) was created by merging the RFC and RNAS, tasked with taking over heavy bombing.

In 1912, some ten miles north north east of Stonehenge another airfield was being built above the village of Upavon, one that could claim to be the first home of the RAF. The station motto was *in principio et semper* - in the beginning and always – and it was here the first night landing was made in 1917. Based around some cavalry training gallops on the edge of Salisbury Plain, when the RAF was founded on 1 April 1918 Upavon became the home of Britain's central flying school, under Commandant Captain Godfrey M Paine, RN. His number two was Major Hugh Trenchard who later became the chief of air staff, and is often referred to as the "father of the Royal Air Force". RAF Upavon ceased to exist in the 1990s but is still an MoD controlled site known as Trenchard Lines, and the officers' mess, built in 1915 and now Grade II* listed , was once the oldest RAF officers' mess still in use.

Despite Trenchard's wishes after the First World War the Stonehenge airfield was deemed surplus to requirements and closed. Despite rumours to the contrary the army never sought to clear the stones, and in fact opened the debate on the value and future of Stonehenge. All hangers had been built to preserve the so-called "sun gap", ensuring the rising sun could be seen from Stonehenge at the summer solstice. In 1927 the Stonehenge protection committee was founded and, with donations from the public, the aerodrome and neighbouring farmland were bought and gifted to the National Trust. By the early 1930s the aerodrome's buildings had all been dismantled and removed.

So the airfield at Stonehenge arguably led to its preservation and a debate about our built heritage. Wiltshire continued to be home to many, many RAF bases, especially during the Second World War. Sparsely populated with open countryside that is often perfect for airfields, Wiltshire was also out of range of German fighters, but only a short flight to our fighter bases in the south east.

RAF Colerne was the biggest air force base in Wiltshire during the Second World War and the list of aircraft based here is a who's who of the era. Spitfires, of course, built at nearby Trowbridge. The original Spitfire factory at Southampton was considered too likely to either be a target or collateral damage from a raid on the docks. Trowbridge built the Mark V to XIV Spitfires including the Griffon powered version. They were transported to Keevil airfield where final assembly took place before female pilots flew them on to their operational bases.

As well as the Spitfire, Wiltshire's RAF bases were also home to such legends as the de Havilland Mosquito, Hawker Hurricane and, post war, the Gloucester Meteor, our first jet fighter. Up in the north of Wiltshire is RAF Fairford, built for the USA air force and RAF aircraft to transport D-Day troops, and the first place Concorde ever landed, on its maiden flight from Filton. Fairford is also home to the world's biggest military air show each July. Everything that can still fly, from Lancasters to the RAF's latest F-35, can be seen.

What was RAF Netheravon is now home to the Joint Services Parachute Centre, including part of the Army's "adventurous training" programme for serving and injured personnel, as well as the Army Parachute Association's charity. It was already being used by the RFC in 1912 and the 1914 officers' mess is Grade II* listed. Historic England rates the buildings at Netheravon as "of outstanding historical interest, and of striking architectural form, comprising some of the earliest extant buildings erected for the RFC". Several other buildings from the era, including five hangars from 1918 are Grade II listed.

Perhaps Wiltshire's most famous airfield was RAF Lyneham, built in 1939 and requiring Lyneham Court manor house, the buildings of Cranley Farm and the village's tennis courts to be cleared. In recent years Lyneham was euphemistically called our "gateway" to Afghanistan, which included flying its C-130 Lockheed Hercules back with those who died there, before they were repatriated via Royal Wootton Bassett. The town is only one of three in the country to be designated Royal, a title awarded after the spontaneous lining of the streets each time repatriated bodies' funeral corteges passed through the town on the way to Oxford.

The first occasion was in April 2007 when town mayor Percy Miles, in full mayoral robes, honoured the first two soldiers, Aaron Lincoln and Danny Wilson, to pass through. On each subsequent occasion the numbers joining him grew, with not just locals but families and others travelling to pay their respects. Impressively the townsfolk kept these congregations entirely apolitical, never judging our involvement in a war but simply showing respect for the fallen.

Before being the home for the RAF's Hercules, Lyneham was also used as a base for the V-bombers when they formed part of our nuclear deterrent. Lyneham is also where Terry Waite returned in 1991 after being held hostage in Beirut, and the RAF's Avro Yorks flew from Lyneham during the Berlin Airlift. This was the operation to supply the western controlled part of the city after the Berlin wall was erected: the RAF's Yorks alone flew in over a million tons of supplies. There is a memorial presented by the senate of Berlin to commemorate the fortieth anniversary of the airlift that started in 1948.

Some of Wiltshire's old airfields have become something quite different: the hangers at RAF Wroughton are used to store the overflowing coffers of the Science Museum, and RAF Hullavington will be where Dyson manufacture their proposed electric car.

The Honda factory north of Swindon is on an old airfield that was part of a Spitfire production facility, but it was after the war that disused airfields would allow England to become a world leader in another area: motor sport. Wiltshire's airfields, like many others, ended the war with nicely finished perimeter tracks that had been used for fuel bowsers and pick up trucks to drive round, servicing aircraft and maintaining security. Now they would make excellent race tracks.

Although the end of hostilities was unequivocally for the good, many who had served found themselves at something of a loss.

They wanted something to replace the camaraderie and adrenalin rush that they had become used to. Car and motorcycle racing around these old perimeter tracks would offer an answer to many.

There were also many manufacturers who needed to publicise their products, and racing would be an ideal platform. During the war motorcycles and cars were built to be robust and reliable, but young men – and the occasional woman – now wanted to add fast to their buying criteria. As well as gaining publicity, manufacturers would also gain valuable development that they had been denied during the war.

Richard Stevens raced for Bradford on Avon's Royal Enfield at what had been RAF Thruxton, once a departure point for gliders used in the D-Day landings. Thruxton in the fastest circuit in the UK, although planning restrictions mean racing is limited and no international races are held there. Despite this the record stands at an average speed of over 113mph on a modified road bike. Back in their glory days Norton had based their race department just outside Thruxton.

RAF Castle Combe also became a race track, with a young Stirling Moss winning an early race. Over the next few years racers such as Colin Chapman, John Surtees and Mike Hailwood would follow, entertaining huge crowds. In Wiltshire alone these old RAF bases, alongside those at Hullavington, Colerne, Keevil and Wroughton would be host to motor racing. And those are just the ones I can remember. So what happened?

Complaints about noise destroyed motorsport at so many venues, usually from people newly arrived to a home they bought in the full knowledge that there was a race circuit nearby. Castle Combe now has such tight restrictions that some standard road bikes cannot be ridden on a track day. When the circuit allowed a six-cylinder Honda like the ones Mike Hailwood raced to be paraded it was between very specific times. At least Wroughton is far enough from anywhere to be the test track in Jeremy Clarkson's *Top Gear* evolution that is shown as *The Grand Tour* by Amazon.

Yet motorsport is worth around £10 billion every year to the British economy, much of it spent on research and development. These are also high skills businesses, offering a career and experience to our brightest engineers. You might ask what it means to the vehicles we actually buy, but electric racing cars and motorcycles are already at the cutting edge of that perennial electric vehicle bugbear of range. Colin Chapman invented the modern car when he realised that a car's bodywork could become its chassis when he brought the monocoque layout of aircraft to cars. Suddenly there was no need for what amounted to a heavy, steel ladder under the car holding everything together: cars could be cheaper, lighter faster and more economical.

The electronics on top end motorcycles and cars are now so advanced that they are banned from racing. Brakes cannot lock and wheels cannot spin when a silicon chip allows you to use maximum grip at all times. Racing has improved the breed so much that some areas need to be reined in so that other limits can be explored.

But this is nothing compared to the technology that now flies above Wiltshire. The Apache attack helicopters that practice their dark arts here have pilots who can read two books at once: it is a trick that comes naturally when you have to fly with one eye peering into a helmet mounted monitor, while the other scans Wiltshire's big skies.

Typhoon fast jet pilots cannot even see their aircraft – cameras and a very expensive helmet mean they can see right through it.

When I sit in the garden watching the RAF's Typhoons put on what I like to think of as my private air show the marvel is that a century ago their predecessors struggled to reach 60mph in the very airspace the Typhoon now races through at ten times that speed. And even that is limited by the outrage a sonic boom would cause if the Typhoon pilot unlocked what is available. This is all technology we have right now even if, just a few decades ago, they would have seemed like flights of fancy.

- NOVEMBER -

PAST PERSECUTIONS

On the 1st November 1943 the residents of Imber, a small village at the heart of Salisbury Plain, were given 47 days' notice to leave. 26 days later the last wedding was held in the village church, St. Giles, and life in the village effectively ended there and then. Often called the forgotten village, it was requisitioned for FIBUA (fighting in built up areas) and used by US forces to prepare for the liberation of the European mainland. I visited as a teenage Air Cadet on a night exercise in the 1970s, saved from capture by a member of our group who was a keep bird watcher and was certain the owl calls were from a species unlikely to be nearby. He was right – it was the army calling out our position, and allowed us to be the only group to get into a building. And then captured, and thrown into the back of a three ton truck with everybody else.

The war office had been buying up Salisbury Plain since Victorian times, initially an area bounded roughly by the Ridgeway, the Devizes to Salisbury Road (A360) and a swathe over to Tidworth. But, as funds and opportunity allowed, they bought more and by 1932 owned land almost as far south as Salisbury and as far west as Westbury and Warminster. This land – including all the property built upon it - was then leased back to tenant farmers and villagers, who would have seen little or no change as a result. But tenants they were and, when the war office needed somewhere for US forces to train for FIBUA, the local Lieutenant Colonel gave everyone in Imber a month to leave.

The notice letter required families who had lived in the village for generations to "vacate by 17 December 1943: we cannot provide alternative accommodation but might try to offer assistance to any villager finding themselves in dire straits."

That was it - the chapel, pub, shop, even recently built council houses were empty within a few weeks. Most people went to stay with family, and some even left furnishings behind, certain they would be allowed to move back in after the war. But it wasn't to be - a public enquiry allowed the MoD free reign, although a subsequent High Court action required the Church to be maintained and opened at least one day a year.

Imber is supposedly open for "up to 50 days in each year" although the MOD hardly shouts it from the rooftops and in practice the number of days granted falls well short of the maximum. Access is usually granted during the Easter and Christmas to New Year periods, and during August. The military training programme supposedly dictates the dates of public access, but these have been getting ever fewer. The ubiquitous "MoD spokesman" announced in June 2017 that "keeping visitors to Imber village safe was a `top priority'" and, expressed concern that people were putting their lives at risk by trespassing into areas where there could be "unexploded ordnance". According to the man from the ministry "we have received numerous reports of members of the public placing themselves and others in danger during previous open days by attempting to access restricted areas. Following these reports a risk assessment was carried out which resulted in the decision to reduce public access periods to the village."

Given that Army Cadets still train in this area, and that a visitor in broad daylight is less likely to step on "unexploded ordnance" than a soldier trying to evade detection in the dead of night, few are convinced that the MoD are being honest. Locals suspect it is just a general ratcheting down in the hope that access can be completely denied at some point in the future. For many of us the fascination is to see a village frozen in time – especially the fabulous church – but for others it is a chance to tend the graves of family members and consider how different their lives might have been.

There are other FIBUA sites on Salisbury Plain, all of which post date war office (now MoD) occupation, some just like Afghan villages, complete with a minaret. Yet Imber remains jealously guarded by the MoD despite relatives of past residents still living locally. All in all, Imber is a moving and affecting place to visit, and it is good to know that it was a useful training base for those brave troops who liberated Europe. It was also invaluable for training those deployed to Northern Ireland during The Troubles, but a little sensitivity would be appreciated by locals who understand that while sometimes needs must, they would like their heritage back now, please. After all it is not as if there is nowhere else to build a training facility, and there has been a settlement at Imber since at least 967.

At least the Grade I listed St Giles' church has been well cared for, and the medieval wall paintings escaped the Victorian "scraping" making it an exceptional historical record. The Victorians hated any decoration in churches, and would scrape plaster and painting off interiors. This was an evolution of our Protestant past: there is even a theory that the outside of Salisbury Cathedral would have been painted red when it was built, something that would not have been tolerated after the Reformation. Funny how Catholic tastes has come to mean simple and unadorned, when for centuries it meant the opposite.

According to legend, St Giles was a seventh century Greek hermit who lived in the forests near Nîmes, in the south of France, with a tame deer as his only companion. The people of Imber probably knew how he felt when they consecrated their church. Although there has been a building of some sort on the site of the church for at least 850 years, much of what is seen today, including the tower, is about 250 years younger – but still 600 years old. The bells came much later, one of the original five dated 1721 now installed at Edington Priory church, a few miles to the north west on the spring line below the Plain. In 2010 St Giles' mixed ring of five bells were joined by a sixth above, mostly nineteenth century, but with one made in 2003. Yes, you can still buy brand new church bells.

British bell ringing is unique and beautiful. The first time I visited Italy and Sunday morning arrived it was as if the townspeople were ringing an alarm – just urgently tugging on a rope in the hope of making as much noise as possible. And it used to be done that way in England as well. Hand bells were originally used to call people to worship, and around 400AD the idea of hanging one in a church was introduced by Paulinus, Bishop of Nola in Campania: hence bell ringing is campanology. Well, maybe - campana is Latin for bell. It was another 200 years or so before the practice of bell ringing reached Britain but, when it did, it would evolve into something magical.

Another special feature of Imber's St Giles' church is that it is one of only two sites in the UK to have bell ringing marks in the tower. These are written on the inside of the bell tower, so that the team of ringers know where they are. That wonderful cadence that carries across the countryside is ultimately known as a peal, taking around three hours to complete.

Because my wife and her family rang in the local church – 50p per wedding, apparently - we were honoured with a quarter peal for our wedding, making the reception in my new in-laws garden, within earshot of the church, even more special.

As someone who has never been a campanologist it is hard to define a peal because there are so many aspects to it. But in essence there must be over 5,000 sequences, or “changes” by the ringers – no, they do not call themselves campanologists – concentrating like mad and following the instructions of the tower captain. Or you could just mark off the changes on the wall, as has been done at Imber.

Oddly this glorious and complex practice came about after the Reformation, with the Catholics having been happy with a rope to swing a bell on a simple spindle. In Britain, by contrast, ringers started experimenting with different ways of hanging bells. By fixing bells to a wheel, with the rope attached to the rim of the wheel, bells could be rung up with a degree of control rather than just crash back and forth. Add a few more bells of different sizes and notes, some like minded ringers, and suddenly you have a musical instrument.

By the 18th century bell ringing was a popular form of exercise with the aristocracy, and could be surprisingly well paid. It is not easy, however, and can be dangerous. You really can be hauled up into the tower and, at a friend’s wedding, my wife almost knocked herself unconscious on the back wall of a small tower with an unfamiliar and poorly prepared bell. If you do not catch the bell in time and let it swing too far it will break a stay putting the bell out of action. So our Catholic cousins have good reason not to copy us.

Our local church practices on a Wednesday evening, and even in November it is wonderful to step outside – to empty the bin, or perhaps lock up the chickens – and hear the bells of St Mary’s church in Market Lavington literally ring out. My wife has to work late on Mondays, but it is mitigated by St James’ church in Devizes, a stone's throw from her surgery, practicing on that evening. It is a joyful sound, even on a dark and wet November night.

The November night is, of course, the fifth. From 1605 church bells – in Anglican churches, of course - rang out every 5th November to remember and celebrate the foiling of a Catholic attempt to blow up King James I and his lords in the hope of securing greater religious tolerance and, ideally, a Catholic monarch. The person who caught Guy Fawkes and his gunpowder was Thomas Knyvet, the first Baron Knyvet, who hailed from Wiltshire. It is a shame that Bonfire Night is now less celebrated since we have fallen so much into the thrall of Hallowe'en, and an American version of Hallowe'en at that. 1st November is All Saints' or All Hallow's day – yes, the day Imber's residents were told to move out – and so the day before is All Hallow's Eve: Hallowe'en.

It gets odd here until you remember we used to count the year differently, and had to shuffle dates around in the eighteenth century to bring the seasons back in line with a written calendar. All Hallow's day was once the start of a new year, 31st October therefore being the last. Or possibly just the end of the farming year. The Romans brought us ten months: October, November and December are simply named after the Latin for months eight, nine and ten. Quiet understandably they thought that winter was a waste of time so did not have a name for the period they later called January and February (after Janus the two faced god who looked back as well as forward, and Februa the feast of purification: yes, a carnival before a fast).

On the last day of the year – Hallowe'en – many believed that the barriers between our world and that of the dead was porous, and a time of great danger. Celtic traditions tell of body paint and carved turnips to ward off evil spirts, and there is your justification to go trick or treating. But the popularity of Hallowe'en is probably more to do with there is so much more that can be sold compared to Guy Fawkes' night.

Remember, remember the fifth of November, traditionally the day to tup sheep in the hope of lambs on April's Fool Day. And also the day Thomas Knyvet, caught Guy Fawkes preparing to destroy the Houses of Parliament. Knyvet hailed from a village called Charlton, in north Wiltshire but is more famous for his London house which was on the site of the current 10 Downing Street.

In a different Wiltshire village called Charlton (a common enough name, meaning charlatan's tun, a tun being a clearing cum farmstead) is Devizes MP Claire Perry, who admitted to setting off a single fuse to launch 20 fireworks, just before singing drifted from a neighbouring church only to drowned out by her pyrotechnics. But at least she was treating her children to an important part of English tradition. Stuffing old clothes with newspaper then trying to raise a "penny for the guy", and building the biggest bonfire possible, used to be an integral part of childhood. Apparently Guy Fawkes' old school, St Peter's in York, refuses to burn a dummy of a former pupil but for the rest of us he is fair game.

But originally the effigy placed on the bonfire was that of the Pope, and November 5th was known as Pope's day in North America. It is hard for us to imagine the bitterness that divided what are, in essence, the same Christian belief. It took the Roman Catholic Relief Act of 1829 to allow all Britons to share certain rights, including sitting in parliament, and it was probably around this period that the effigy became Guy Fawkes rather than the Pope. Even so, November 5th remained a public holiday until 1859.

Such was the persecution of anybody who attempted to hold a Catholic Mass, Catholic priests were hidden away in houses in what became known as priest holes. These could even involve building an extension designed especially to hide a holy man. One such space in a Wiltshire village was found to contain a skeleton during renovations, and historian Melanie Backe-Hansen speculated that the owners were arrested leaving their priest unable to escape.

Burning effigies of the Pope in that sort of world made perfect sense.

Children sitting in the street by their guy would ask for a penny from each passer, hoping to raise money for fireworks. Despite the ruinous inflation of the 1930s and 1970s we were still asking for no more than that when I was a kid. Today Bonfire Night might not involve a bonfire at all, but rather a spectacular firework display beloved of schools and other charities as a fundraiser. These rattle on right through November, desperately trying not to clash with other displays while terrifying animals for a full four weeks. Rather quieter is the spectacular Festival of Lights at Longleat that runs from November to the New Year, bringing in Chinese artists to tell a different story each year. As the nights get ever longer heading towards the winter solstice it is shows such as this that turn the darkness into a celebration, ready for the biggest party of the year, hopefully moving on from past persecutions.

AMERICAN ROA

- DECEMBER -

FEAST

Nearly there. The C-word that is. To be honest, I have never really liked Christmas. But the food! This is England at its best. For too long it has been fashionable to knock English cooking but that was really a hangover from post war rationing and school dinners. In truth we have some of the best ingredients and purest cooking style. Our climate is perfect for growing grass, and the chalk downs and plain of Wiltshire are good for little else. So we have finest free range meat available to us, spiced up if needs be with everything our Empire brought back.

The quality of our meat also allowed it to be cooked simply and speedily. Even the French noticed, calling us *rosbifs* (roast beefs). Some has suggested this is because we get sunburnt on holiday, but that is it is not true according to linguistics expert Professor Richard Coates of Sussex University. Talking to the BBC he confirmed the nickname *rosbif* came about in the 18th century due to the English style of cooking beef. The French, by contrast tended to either fry the better cuts, or make stews.

English cooking also lacks what the Italians call *cucina povera* – kitchen of the poor. The further south in Italy you go, the more this is noticeable. Health experts agree it is very good for you – if you can get enough of it – comprising simple dishes that involve lots of vegetables and salad, supplemented by a little oily fish. By the time you get to Sicily it is mainly carbohydrates eking out what little protein can be found: the national dish is pasta con sarde: sardines, chilli, pine nuts, fennel and raisins. These are things you can gather (or dry grapes to create) and if you had no luck fishing it is called "the sardines escaped". In England the equivalent would be something like Yorkshire pudding, served as a first course with the onions roasted alongside the beef. But then you still have the roast beef to come.

Northern Italy is very different to the south, and often features dishes an Englishman would recognise: chops, and sausages are typical, although usually served alone with vegetables as a separate course. Maybe they enjoy washing up. Caterina de' Medici took this style of cooking to France when she toured the country, despite (or perhaps because – royal families loved a spot of networking via marriage) her father being the ruler of Florence. When in 1613, aged 14, she married the future King Henry II of France the French were initially wowed by the food and chefs Caterina brought with her. But gradually the King's chef added flourishes that horrified Italians. "I mean", they (might have) said, "cream with meat? Really?" Ironically the French are still bemused by us *rosbifs* having "jam with meat". Apple sauce, redcurrant jelly, Cumberland sauce: that sort of thing.

A roast is always a celebration. Brought to the table to be carved a roast is a rejoicing of companionship, a companion being someone you break bread with (from the Italian *con pane*: with bread). And Christmas dinner is the greatest of all the roasts. In a way it was invented by the people who built Stonehenge as they feasted on the winter solstice.

4000 years ago it seems that Stonehenge was *the* place to be buried, and it is possibly the biggest human burial ground of its era. None of the human remains show signs of violent death, and most are healthy, implying people of status and power. Later burials are cremations, the remains of bones painstakingly reassembled by researchers. Given that it is estimated half a tonne of timber would have been needed for each cremation, and that no evidence of cremations has been found locally, it seems these burials were akin to our state funerals. The remains of cremated human bones, all mixed together, were discovered in the Aubrey pits (the places where missing stones or timber posts were noted) and the people who were buried here may have links to the parts of western Wales where the bluestones came from. It seems a cremation ceremony must have been held some distance from Stonehenge and then the remains of the skeleton brought, probably with a great sense of occasion, to the stones. A Westminster cathedral of its day? We may never know.

The how of Stonehenge is better understood, and just as remarkable as the why. Around 4000 years ago the first stone circle - now the inner circle - of small bluestones were erected, then abandoned. It is pretty settled that they were brought from the Prescelly Mountains in southwestern Wales via waterways for the most part. Eighty stones, weighing some four tonnes each, took a 240 mile journey for reasons we can only guess at.

The big sarsen stones of the outer circle came from the area around Avebury, some twenty miles to the north, but given they weigh up to fifty tonnes a piece moving them was an equally astounding feat. Again, transport on water seems possible. The River Avon – at Durrington Walls, where the builders of Stonehenge lived – runs to Upavon and a minor tributary then runs north west to Marden where there was a smaller henge. From here it is possible to chart a comparatively level course to Avebury and the land of the sarsen stones.

Durrington Walls was, at the time Stonehenge was built, by far the biggest centre of population in Europe. It has been suggested that as many as a thousand buildings once stood around Durrington Walls, and that people here lived into their fifties and possibly beyond. That Wiltshire was so densely populated and a centre not just for England but also mainland Europe makes the fact it is so comparatively empty today a mystery. That so many people came together to build such spectacular monuments would be astounding today. Were they slaves, fed easily caught and cooked meat rather than a more varied diet of prepared food? After all, other great wonders such as the pyramids and the colosseum in Rome were built by slaves. Yet there is no evidence of slavery during this period in Wiltshire so perhaps it was just driven by an awe of what people working together could achieve, and how important the seasons had become now that we were farmers. Unusually for the period, remains suggest Stonehenge's creators' diet was mostly meat, rather than grain based as was common at the time. The pigs they feasted on fed perhaps 4,000 people living in circumstances we would recognise.

We do not know much of the why of Stonehenge or its people – we do not know anything of their language, or if they kept records – but we know of the alignments for the summer and winter solstice especially. We also know that the stars are in pretty much the same place in our night sky as they were when Stonehenge was built. Although it is the summer solstice that is most celebrated today, and would have been useful for planning a harvest, the winter solstice is far more important to farmers. After all, it is obvious when a crop is ready to bring in, but judging when to plant seed, start to mate livestock and retrieve your pigs from the woods is harder to judge.

The best guesses about Stonehenge are getting tantalisingly close to what is likely to be the truth, thanks in part to the examination of the thousands of domestic pig bones buried at a time when

Stonehenge was one of the busiest places on earth. All the pigs were slaughtered at around nine months old which, given a spring birth, means for the winter solstice. Some came from north east Scotland(!) a journey of at least a month on foot. Others came from south Wales, the rest from pretty much every corner of England. So it seems Stonehenge's earliest message was: "We're having a winter solstice party! Bring a pig!"

You can imagine the early Christians looking at the solstice celebrations and wondering how they were going to hijack such a party. The Romans celebrated the winter solstice between the 17th and 23rd and chose 25th December as Christmas Day, even though most academics agree spring or autumn are more likely candidates if you want to find the day Jesus Christ was born. Given the reputation the Romans had for feasting perhaps they were just trying to drag a party out by an extra couple of days.

The original meat for English feasts, including Christmas, was venison from wild deer. Lower orders might be allowed the numbles – the internal organs. Numbles is one of those words that confused early English printers into creating the prefix "an" rather than a: so a numble was printed as an umble. They were sometimes made into a pie for the lower orders in a household, who had to eat umble pie. We say humble pie now, but the roots of the two words are different. By 1600 the recipe included bacon, and in 1662 Samuel Pepys' diary entry included "I having some venison given me a day or two ago, and so I had a shoulder roasted, another baked, and the umbles baked in a pie, and all very well done." Then, almost exactly a year later he wrote that "Mrs Turner came in and did bring us an umble pie hot out of her oven, extraordinarily good."

The sheer number of deer around us means that our dog often has to remain on a lead. Ziggy is a black and tan lurcher, a breed often dismissed as a poacher's dog by pedigree owners. Many centuries ago only noblemen were allowed to keep dogs bred for deer hunting, the original sport of English kings. Behind Devizes castle – a Victorian residential redevelopment on the original Norman foundations – is a surprisingly original deer park. These were built with deep earth banks art their boundary, too high for a deer to leap and too steep to climb. But even more ingenious was the outside of the banks, which were gentle steps that encouraged deer from the surrounding forest to find their way into the park.

So venison became the preserve of noblemen, but that did not stop the rest of us coveting it. Deerhounds and similar breeds were the preserve of those entitled to hunt deer, so there quickly became a demand for a dog that common people could legally own that could bring down a deer. These lurchers – there is no recognised breed – are mongrels that are not big enough to raise suspicion as to their real purpose, but when acting as a pair can easily bring down even large deer. Running alongside their prey at more than 30 mph, the first hound will flick themselves into the flank of a running deer: the equivalent of throwing a sack of potatoes from a moving vehicle. The hapless deer goes down and is despatched by the second dog ripping out its throat. The first lurcher will stand guard, barking to call its owner. Neither dog would dream of trying to eat their prey.

Perhaps the most terrifying thing, after a thousand years of breeding, is that lurchers do not need to be trained to do this. When Ziggy was just six or seven months old he floored me by throwing himself sideways at me during a bout of puppy madness. Lurchers put everything into being fast and furious: reputedly even their hearing is turned off during a chase. Thin skin and sparse fur make for speed and sizable vets bill when something weighing 25 kg travelling at 35 mph disappears into a hedge that harbours old barbed wire.

Yet lurchers are incredibly binary, a Ferrari as a couch potato. As long as they are allowed their zoom time, for 23 hours a day they will just flop. They are astonishingly loyal, affectionate and even tempered. Even pinning Ziggy down for the vet, there has never been a suggestion he might bite something. Unless he was trying to catch that something.

It is increasingly odd that people who eat meat are so squeamish about hunting. 97% of the chicken eaten in Britain lived a miserable life, allocated a space about the size of a sheet of A4 paper. It shares its floodlit life with thousands of equally unhappy birds, fighting for what little space it has with a beak that has been trimmed to save it from damaging the flesh of itself or others. Much imported pork and piggy based treats are from animals that lived in a space they could not turn round in. Even the hunted fox had a better life before its final, admittedly terrifying, hour or so. The beef from our local butcher is no more expensive than a supermarket but grazes in the Wiltshire countryside, and shelters in a barn on locally grown silage during the worst of winter.

The tradition of a roast bird as a centrepiece started with swan, famously only allowed to be eaten with the consent of the monarch. Chicken was more expensive than goose, which was the default setting for most people's Christmas feast. Even after turkey was introduced from America – apparently first eaten by Henry VIII – goose remained the pauper's choice, famously about to be served by Bob Cratchit until Ebenezer Scrooge bought him a turkey. There is far more meat on a typical turkey than on a goose, and far less fat. A friend cursed the day he was given a goose because it took almost a day to clean the oven after roasting it.

A little over a mile from us as the crow flies is the Sharp family's West Park farm, with, for the most part, Friesian dairy cattle. These are part of a typical Wiltshire traffic calming scheme, as the road needs to be blocked to allow the cows to move between the milking parlour and their grazing. Even when you are late watching Daisy and company amble along, occasionally trying out the grass on the verge, is surprisingly therapeutic.

But, like most farms, if another family member wants to join in, diversification is the key. So Oliver Sharp has a huge barn where his bronze turkeys get ready for Christmas. True free range is difficult, not just because of foxes but also weasels and stoats that lurk in Parham wood. The birds have room to roam around a spacious, modern barn, slowly maturing and most importantly, kept happy. They are hand plucked to avoid the grizzly cuts and bruises of machine striped poultry and hung for 10 days to develop flavour. They taste fantastic and, if not as cheap as the frozen supermarket variety, cost a third of what the fancy foodie outlets charge for a goose.

Buying meat is also not just about price versus taste. Welfare is talked about, but rarely touches on the journey animals take to their final destination. There is also the environmental impact of moving stuff around, with all those trucks thundering up and down the country. And an aside: hauliers will regularly claim that HGVs do not cause damage to roads because they apply no more pressure to the Tarmac per square inch/metre/whatever than a family car. This is either disingenuous, or proves they do not understand hydraulics. I hope it is the former.

Sugar was the next big thing in feasting, a controversial ingredient now, but not half as controversial as how it was made. Our desire for a foothold in what is now the United States was driven by the need to supply the islands where slaves worked on the sugar plantations. There are some impressive houses and much more in Wiltshire built on the profits of our darkest hour. That we were the first to free slaves might be judged by the fact that we were the first to experience an industrial revolution at pretty much the same time slavery was abolished in Britain. That we were taught slavery by the people of north Africa, who would raid churches on our south coast on Sundays, can be no excuse. But we are where we are, and that includes the sugar genie.

The Elizabethans loved sugar, holding a cube between their teeth and sipping tea through it. Unsurprisingly it rotted their teeth, but that did not stop them adding it to everything, including meat: mincemeat really did start out as just that until all that was left was the beef suet – the fat around the kidneys – that is still in most mince pies.

Oh, and pies. Is there anything more English? Although some claim they are of Greek origin, pies (or pyes, as once written) appeared in the 12th century. Originally the pastry was not eaten, but used as a carrier for the filling or as decoration. The nursery rhyme *four and twenty blackbirds* tells all about that, and how songbirds were once a delicacy, with Samuel Pepys already telling us how good even umble pie could be.

The recipe for Devizes pie tells how nothing was wasted: the filling included thin slices of "cold calf's head with some of the brains, pickled tongue, sweetbreads, lamb, veal, a few slices of bacon, and hard-boiled eggs... in layers into a pie-dish, with plenty of seasoning between each, of cayenne, white pepper, all-spice and salt... rich gravy; cover it with a flour and water paste; bake it in a slow oven, and when perfectly cold, take off the crust, and turn the pie out upon a dish; garnish it with parsley and pickled eggs cut into slices".

Wiltshire pork pie added bacon, cheese, onion and apple to a pork belly filling, seasoned with pepper and sage: a very different filling to modern pork pies. It was probably something workers took into the fields, rather like the Cornish miners took pasties.

The finest savoury pie surely has to be raised game pie. The pastry is made with lard (pork fat), flour and hot water. The pastry case is filled with game (whatever you have shot - or poached) plus a fatty pork cut, diced or minced, to prevent the naturally lean game becoming dry and tough. Oh, and bacon (of course) with a gravy made using that English favourite Madeira. This has been a centrepiece to serve cold in England for centuries, and makes a fabulous addition to the Boxing Day cold cut feast that must rank as the best meal of the year. Served with chutney, something so English it could only have come from India. Perhaps with some buttered baked potatoes, although initially people refused to eat potatoes because, judging from the flowers, they feared spuds might be related to deadly nightshade – which they are. They only became popular when people realised you could have a pitched battle in a potato field without damaging the crop. The same does not apply to wheat.

Wiltshire had its own cheeses, but with Somerset making so much Cheddar just over the border most of them have been forgotten. An aside: the term ploughman's lunch was invented by the Milk Marketing Board years ago to try and sell more cheese. And in the early days ploughs were usually shared between members of a community so, while people might have taken bread and cheese into the field, it is unlikely it was reserved for the ploughmen. Or, indeed the time when the fields were ploughed.

The plough is often cited as the most important human invention of them all. Evidence of its early use is all over Wiltshire in the so-called strip lynchets, terraces formed as a plough went back and forward across the slopes of the Downs. An acre was originally defined as the area a man could plough in a day, and would have varied depending on soil, plough and what was pulling it. Eventually it was settled at 220 yards by 22 yards, the latter being the length of a cricket pitch. Is that really a coincidence?

Switching to a grain based diet might not have been healthy – the new farmers' hunter gatherer forebears were taller and seemingly healthier – but it did feed a lot of mouths. This meant that perhaps only one person in four or five was needed to provide food while everybody else could go off and do other things. Unfortunately this often involved war, trying to be the person in charge, and generally being Machiavellian. It is a shame we could not have just wandered around philosophising as the Greeks did. Well, some of them. Perhaps the English just needed to do something to keep themselves warm. Like build Stonehenge, abandoning bread during the winter solstice and cooking all those piglets for the ultimate feast.

- AFTERWORD -

Growing up in Wiltshire in the late sixties and early seventies I witnessed the technological and economic changes that altered farming and village life beyond recognition, but it happened away from the public eye. Automatic milking equipment, conveyor belts for stacking hay bales, combine harvesters and such drastically reduced the number of people needed on a farm. When the same changes came to the industrialised midlands and north there was mayhem, followed by partisan fury from the newspapers. But in the country, as new equipment arrived and farms merged to create economies of scale, no one noticed. Perhaps governments and consumers (although we were customers back then) liked the lower prices, but it hollowed out the Wiltshire landscape. Tied cottages were lost, and people who had only know the land moved to a local town, unable to afford the prices incomers could pay, even back then. The village shops disappeared, and are being followed by the post offices and pubs. People stopped knowing each other, and only now are events such as the Urchfont Scarecrow festival and Andy Scott's Rock against Cancer concerts are making amends. It has not been lost on people here that when governments did try and (eventually) make amends for the human cost of massive changes in cities and industrial areas, the country has always been studiously ignored. Public transport, if you want the Stonehenge tour of Salisbury Plain, is almost glamourous, if expensive. But if you just want a bus home from Salisbury, you had better finish work by 5pm sharp. Unless, as is often the case the bus has broken down. There are few, if any, busses on Sundays.

And yet country folk are sanguine about being ignored, for the most part. People just accept that's the way it is, in the same way they accept you need a decent coat in winter. And it could be worse: cities and towns are being homogenised by chains of retailers and restaurants, and their outskirts by housing development.

The only really noticeable changes to Wiltshire's countryside in the last fifty years have been the grubbing up of hedges, the loss of elm trees and the ubiquitous yellow fields of rape. And the weather – people in the country notice the weather. The snowdrops were late this year, but the bluebells were early. Orange tipped butterflies appeared on cue, as did the blackbird song. The lack of rain, witnessed by the water levels in ditches and ponds, is worrying although the mild nights mean the pear and apple blossom should set to fruit unless there is a late frost.

People in towns and cities are busy noticing an endless succession of must see movies and plays, must own fashion, must visit destinations. A treadmill that will never end, unless capitalism eats itself. The countryside is cyclical, with a never ending repetition of an apparently repeated story: but if you notice things, and if you are prepared to look and take an interest, is subject to endless variation and surprises. Funnily enough one treatment for anxiety and depression, mindfulness, encourages just that: taking time to step back and notice things. Maybe that is why country folk do not get worried about being ignored.

And they certainly do not ignore each other. Passing one another will involve at least a wave, if not a full blown 20 minute gossip. But gossip will include commenting on such things as sunsets, clear night skies, and how winter seems to have become a dull waiting room for spring, rather than the clearly defined season when frosts would break down ploughed fields and sterilize pig sties. Country people notice small things, and value them. This would be called cognitive behavioural therapy in a city, and the Human Henge project, helping mental illness sufferers by offering guided walking tours around Stonehenge, is formalising the practice. Yes, that Stonehenge, the one in Wiltshire. But now you know that. So consider yourself ready to enjoy a slice of this most nuanced, historic and varied part of heaven on earth.

THANKS & ACKNOWLEDGEMENTS

First, a thank you to my beautiful wife Joanna for allowing me the time and money to produce this book. Oh, and the cruel but fair proofing…

Grateful appreciation to Chris Combe and Roy Kyte, one used to farming on a fairly large scale, the other not, for their insight into the realities of farming. And thanks to Andrew McInereney for telling what it is like to train on Salisbury Plain.

Thank you also to Peter Buckman of the Ampersand Agency for encouragement to self-publish, and Jim Gill for his advice.

I read voraciously, everything from cereal boxes upwards, so there are many books that may have planted seeds to content in this story. But in particular I can commend:

Wiltshire Folklore by Kathleen Wiltshire ISBN 978-0859550161

The Little Book of Wiltshire by Dee La Vadera ISBN 978-0752469935

Flying with the Larks by Timothy C Brown ISBN 978-0752489896

A Shepherd's Life by WH Hudson ISBN 978-1530015511

The Folklore of Wiltshire Ralph Whitlock ISBN 978-0874717723

And wherever interests you in Britain, the relevant Pevsner's guide should be on your bookshelf

The illustrations that open chapters are Schluss Vignetten Dingbats by Dieter Steffmann. The sketch on the right is by Eve Pullen, the rest my photographs via Photoshop. The main cover font is augie by Steven J Lundeen and the white horse based upon an image by lineart@shy-fox.

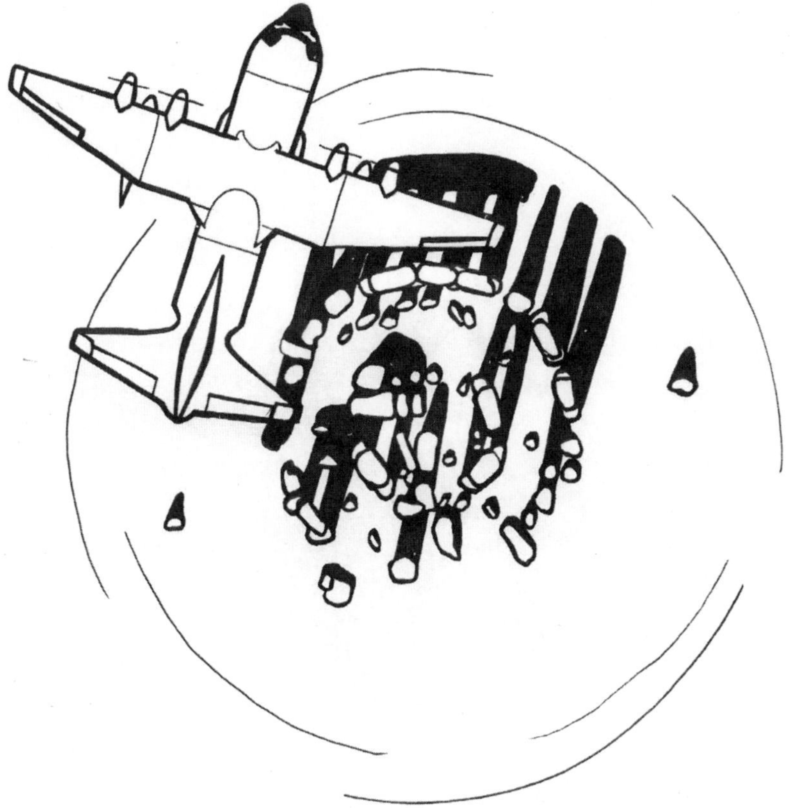